Savin Rock

An Illustrated History
2nd Edition

by

Bennett W. Dorman

Photo Restoration & Design
North Haven, Connecticut

Published by
Photo Restoration & Design
46 Marlborough Road
North Haven, CT 06473
(203) 230-9137

ISBN 0-9669159-0-9

Printed by Rollins Printing, Hamden, Ct.

All photos in this book are from the Author's collection unless otherwise noted.
The first photo is from Harold Hartmann's Collection.

DEDICATION

To the memory of the many entrepreneurs, workers and patrons
who made the Savin Rock Amusement Park the Coney Island of
Connecticut for nearly one hundred years.

And

To my wife, Catherine, and daughter, Diane, whose steadfast
confidence in this project encouraged and enabled me to make my
dream of a pictorial history of Savin Rock a reality.

PREFACE

Why did I feel a compulsion to put on the market a book of Savin Rock pictures? There were many reasons. As a youngster, I lived at a seaside paradise called Prospect Beach, perhaps a half mile west of the Rock area. During the season, we would take spur of the moment walks to enjoy the sights, sounds and smells of the grand old park. As we boys grew into teen-agers and developed an interest in girls, we would take them there for a ride on the carousel and perhaps a hot dog or frozen custard. There was never enough money in those Depression years to do much else except to walk around, but the girls understood.

I had already written two short histories of the Rock which had some old pictures, but received many requests for a book with more pictures -- especially from viewers of the many free slide shows I gave through the years. The constant requests were flattering, but did not inflate my energy as I was nearing eighty.

Then I met Denise Smith, my publisher, and she proved to be the catalyst for this endeavor. Telling me how much she enjoyed my very last slide show, she urged me to become her partner in this venture and bestowed enough of her energy on me to get me started. Her talent in restoring faded and torn photos, her business acumen and drive are all readily apparent and she's become a good friend to my wife, Catherine, my daughter, Diane and me.

Bennett W. Dorman

TABLE OF CONTENTS

~~~~~~

FORWARD 6

ACKNOWLEDGMENTS 7

INTRODUCTION 8

CHAPTER ONE................... THE WAY WE WERE 11

CHAPTER TWO...................THE WAY WE REMEMBER 77

CHAPTER THREE...............THE WAY WE ARE .185

CHAPTER FOUR.................AMONG OUR SOUVENIRS 235

MRS. EDWARD H. NORTH
CITY HISTORIAN
77 Center Street
West Haven, Connecticut 06516
Telephone 933-2684

WARD-HEITMAN HOUSE

Bennett Dorman's Illustrated History of Savin Rock Amusement Parks will be of momentous interest to those who experienced enjoyable visits there.

Through his pictures Mr. Dorman escorts us on a memorable tour of a long-ago magical land.

His book is an authentic pictorial history of a very special place in West Haven's past. It will surely become a well documented reference for future historians.

Harriet C. North
City Historian

ACKNOWLEDGMENTS

My heartfelt thanks to all who helped me in any way to prepare this amusement park anthology. My gratitude compels me to name my fellow members of "Club 90" who provided me with the history of both people and places and helped me in remembering it all. They are (alphabetically) Henry Dreher, Harold Hartmann, Ex-West Haven Mayor Bob Johnson, Bill Kaminski, Ed Kearns, Bill Levere, Ron and Russ Levere, Pat Libero, Connie Pace, Joe Santora and Doctor Hugh Taurchini. And in memoriam: John Clemence, Charles "Bud" Harger, Roland Larrivee, Ed Levere, Fred Levere and Maynard "Lin" Lindsay.

My limitless thanks to Denise Smith of Photo Restoration and Design who, with her skills in her art and her record keeping as my publisher, kept everything on an "even keel" but, in particular, her solicitude and calming influence when various things went awry as they sometimes do in any publishing endeavor.

My sincere thanks to Richard Hodes, a most talented West Haven artist, who gratuitously granted use of his work of art featured on the jacket of this book.

To Kathy O'Keefe Ceravone, who graciously answered a last minute call for extra computer help, my heartfelt gratitude.

And to all those who permitted their treasured photographs of a bygone era to be reproduced here and to the many who allowed images of their Savin Rock artifacts to be displayed on these pages, I give my grateful thanks.

Bennett (Bill) Dorman

A SPECIAL THANKS to the members of Club 90 for allowing Photo Restoration & Design to create the first Savin Rock Calendar to be sold for the purpose of helping to offset printing and production costs for this book.

To the owners and employees of West Haven's Brian's Place, Duffy's Tavern, Savin Rock Antiques and Hamden's Rollins Printing, for promoting and selling our calendars for us.

To Muriel Blaze and her staff at Barnes and Noble of Orange, Connecticut, for hosting two events for the promotion of our calendars and this book. The success of those events helped us to achieve our goal.

To Donald Wrinn and the members of the Rotary Club for having us as their special guests to promote this book.

To CyberChrome of Branford for their help in large scanning.

To our friends at the Oxford Fire Department for their support and loan of a 16mm projector used to restore an original film of Savin Rock to be viewed on our web site.

To Bob Tracy for adding our Savin Rock web site to West Haven's web site, and for promoting our calendars.

To the owners and employees of MGM Instruments for allowing me the time I needed to complete this project.

To my three children for taking over daily tasks for me during the final months of this project.

And to Ed Kearns for believing in me. His unwavering devotion, support and encouragement has made this book possible.

Denise A. Smith

INTRODUCTION

The seed of the evolution of Savin Rock Park is generally considered by local historians to have been a ten-room edifice called Allen's Tavern. Earlier historians claim it was there as early as 1771. At any rate, it was there when the British invaded our shores on July 5, 1779 and old chronicles tell us that they took over the tavern after landing. One man, though, was the catalyst behind the dream that became the Savin Rock mostly remembered. He was George Kelsey, a dynamic owner of two West Haven factories who, in the 1860s, foresaw the possibilities of making the area into something more than a "watering hole." He was responsible for the first horsecar line in 1867 between New Haven and West Haven and he had it travel down Campbell Ave., then west down Beach St. However, after the first blush of success the novelty wore off and the number of riders decreased.

Undaunted, Kelsey ordered built a grand establishment he called the Sea View House (later changed to Hotel), a bandstand and fountain in near proximity, an observation tower and a sturdy 1,500 foot pier — all this begun in 1870.

These ventures drew the attention of other entrepreneurs and soon there were such things as a portable carousel, gravity railway (a sort of Mill Chutes without water) and other diversions to keep Kelsey's horsecar line solvent.

With the advent of electricity in West Haven in 1892, the horses were retired in 1893 and the electric trolleys took over. Instead of going down Beach Street, they swung west down Thomas Street and entered the "loop" area, between Grove and Summer Streets and were able to discharge their passengers at covered waiting stations between Railroad Grove and what in 1903 became White City. After unloading, they "made the loop" and returned to New Haven. The Winchester R.R. Company owned the "loop" area until it eventually became part of the Connecticut Company which had lines running throughout the state.

When Kelsey started his projects in 1870, he bought the old baseball field between Beach and Palace Streets just west of the Sea View House and moved it north into the area that later became White City. The ball park was then moved again, this time about two blocks west where it eventually became host to not only baseball but football, auto-racing and track meets.

After the turn of the century, sideshows were very popular and there was greater diversification in the rides. One of them was a ferryboat ride across the sound to Lighthouse Point, East Haven, where, if one chose, a trolley ride back to New Haven was possible.

During the teens and twenties, Savin Rock (or just the "Rock") was exceedingly popular with many public bathhouses catering to bathers, baseball to watch on Sunday afternoons by Pop, while Mom traipsed around the amusements with the kids. For the younger romantically inclined adults, there was the Palais Royale with orchestras like Barney Rapp's to dance to (his brother, Barry Wood, later was a regular singer on radio's "Lucky Strike Hit Parade") and Yale's Rudy Vallee could be heard and seen crooning through his megaphone (no mikes in those days).

After the stock market crash in 1929 when money became tight, the Rock became a somewhat different place. People who, heretofore, came to have a family shore dinner, now came to look at the crowd and munch on a five cent hot dog or maybe a nickel frozen custard.

However, after a couple of years of economic readjusting, people came to see a new national craze — the dance marathons. The dancers performed (usually by singing) and broadcast most nights over a local radio station. It was fairly easy to tell what stage of the marathon they were in by their singing voices — when they sounded like frogs, one knew the event was nearly over. One Frank Lovecchio won it in 1933 with his partner, Ruth Johnstone — some may know him by his later alias Frankie Laine. At another, we were lucky to have a young, relatively unknown as M.C. — Red Skelton.

The Depression didn't necessarily keep people away from the Rock. It was great escapism for many to just forget economics and "see and do something."

There were some entrepreneurs who didn't make it down there in those years, but a surprising number did. Toward the end of the thirties people had something to fret about besides the Depression — the drums of Hitler's war were getting louder. Your scribe remembers his intended father-in-law, a retired career navy man, telling all who would listen that the place to watch out for was the Pacific.

The Rock held its own during the war and can thank the trolleys, in part, because while many of us were working in jobs relative to the war effort and making pretty good money, gas rationing precluded much use of our cars for pleasure driving. The old open trolleys to the Rock in the summer were well populated and folks could go to the Rock or just beyond to Donovan Field to watch a talented local baseball team (implemented by some big league players with false names) take on all comers.

After the boys and gals arrived from wartime duties, it seemed for a while that things were back to normal at the Rock. The returnees seemed to be enjoying the Rock's special ambiance for a while but after a year or so crowds seemed smaller again. One got the impression that they were trying hard to have the "same good old time" but had perhaps matured mentally beyond their one-time youthful exuberance for such ephemeral pleasures as an amusement park offered. Many, of course, married and had an investment in a new home in one of a myriad of new tracts in suburbia and worked two jobs to enable them to fulfill mortgage commitments, leaving little loose change for amusement.

Another problem was parking. People with cars wanted to use them. The trolleys, which had served the public for so many years, now seemed archaic what with waiting for them, having to oftentimes transfer to another to get somewhere and then having to repeat the procedure, with the added feature of sometimes rowdy and jostling patrons on the return trip.

Most families owned a car and preferred them for their trips to the Rock but the parking facilities, barely adequate in prewar days, became almost entirely inadequate in the immediate postwar years. There was some available street parking but when the town installed parking meters, most folks out for a few hours enjoyment had to worry about finding their car adorned with a parking violation ticket. There were few parking lots of any size in the area and a few private homes allowed parking on their premises — for a fee, of course.

The Savin Rock Business Men's Association, established in 1911, trying to protect their vested interests, arranged for busloads of people to travel from various outlying areas to spend a day at the Rock. However, in reality, it became evident that the busses were taking up too much of the available parking space normally used by autos. Moreover, due to inadequate public sanitary facilities, the people were "making do" with the space between busses for their needs. This, of course, created an odoriferous aura in the area which was another nail in the coffin of the Grand Old Lady known as Savin Rock.

As the 1950s wound down, it was becoming readily apparent that the Rock was, perhaps, on its last legs — and it was.

The 1960s saw the wake of the old girl and the burial rites were finished by 1968 when the last building became a heap of rubble.

Developers, of course, have been trying to get their feet in the door with grandiose plans for twelve story high-rise apartments, marinas, more restaurants, etc., but so far have been thwarted by the local citizenry through S.O.S. (Save our Shore), IMPACT (Independent Movement for Positive Action) and the current Land Trust of West Haven, Inc. These three entities have been fighting to keep the shorefront open, without any commercialism for thirty years (backed by thousands of bonafide signatures of residents) but still have not been given an asked for protection easement.

To those of us who remember the Rock, it was a very special and wonderful place, full of gaiety, hoarse-voiced barkers, refreshment stands filled with the aroma of french fries and popcorn and, best of all, the rides, when we could afford them.

This volume should take you along Beach St. with its beautiful views of Long Island Sound, through the Upper and Lower Groves to the Trolley Waiting Stations and, across the tracks, the beloved section called White City. Transport yourself back in time — read — and if you enjoy it, keep anticipating Volume II.

CHAPTER ONE

~~~~~~~~~

THE WAY WE WERE

View of Savin Rock's Shoreline, looking northeast from Savin Rock Proper at lower left to the 1st Avenue sandbar at far right. circa 1937. Part of George Kelsey's 1500 ft. pier is shown. An 1880s storm had already shortened it considerably and the hurricane of September 21, 1938 destroyed most of the rest of it.

Harold Hartman's Collection

Hill's Homestead (formerly Allen's Tavern) the oldest entity at Savin Rock.

The evolution of Savin Rock as an oasis and future amusement center began about 1771 with the opening of Allen's Tavern, a ten-room inn where a room could be rented for fifteen cents a night with free use of the cooking ovens. Located on a rutty road, which later became Beach Street, it was a gathering place for sailors, fishermen, travelers and veterans of the Revolutionary War. The word "cocktail" is said to have originated here when a rooster's tail feather from one of the inn's brood inadvertently dropped into the glass of a British officer. The drink was then dubbed a "cocktail." So says a New Haven Register article of 3-15-66 that goes on to say that during his term of office, President Chester Arthur stayed there as did the then heavyweight boxing champ, the "Boston Strong Boy," John L. Sullivan.

In 1850, Aldrend and James Hill (known as the Hill brothers) purchased the old Allen's Tavern and named it "Hill's Homestead." Gradually gaining prestige, Hill's was considered to be the "Newport" of Connecticut. Acquired many years later by John St. Lawrence who retained the name, it was relocated a few blocks east of the elegant brick Anderson home on the corner of Peck Avenue. This was a temporary measure while the original building was being renovated. In its last years before demolition, the old homestead was acquired by Bob Tiernan who changed the name to Tiernan's Old Homestead. It numbered among many of its famous guests such names as Casey Stengel, George Weiss, Jimmy Durante and Bob Hope.

The Savin Rock House dates back to 1838 and was the second oldest entity at Savin Rock. Located just east of Savin Rock Proper, set on 20 acres and large enough for 100 or more overnight guests. The Savin Rock House was destroyed by fire in 1870.

The Savin Rock House was located at the western end of Beach Street just east of Savin Rock Proper. Erected in 1838, it was the second hostelry of consequence to be built in the area, and was one of the largest ever built along the shorefront. It had 100 rooms and was a well-known rendezvous of the wealthy.

The Savin Rock House was originally run by A. A. Upson and S. R. Hotchkiss, who soon sold their vested interest to J. H. and T. H. Dawe, who placed one Samuel H. Crane in the managerial position.

Set on 20 acres, it boasted every conceivable recreational facility available at that time such as salt water bathing, horseback riding, archery, bowling and billiards to mention a few. The cuisine was excellent and varied, served in the spacious dining room or in private rooms. There were lounges, well appointed with comfortable easy chairs for the elderly or indolent of nature. For the more spirited, there was always an orchestra to dance to.

The Savin Rock House was served by the Horse Railroad beginning in 1867. The tracks of this railroad ended on Beach Street near what was later called the Sea View Hotel, built about 1870. A small shelter was built at this point for visitors and guests. Management of the Savin Rock House provided its own stage called the "Flying Cloud" to bring patrons as well as supplies to its door.

The following is a description of the Savin Rock House from Benham's New Haven Directory and Annual Advertiser for 1867-68 New Haven: Printed and published by J. H. Benham, 1867:

> Located four miles below the city, on the west side, is a bluff of rocks which takes its name from the savin, or evergreen shrub, which formerly abounded here. Immediately adjacent to the rock is the finest beach for bathing to be found on the Connecticut shore. From time immemorial this has been a place of popular resort for parties from the surrounding countryside.

A small boarding house was erected here some years since, which passed through the hands of successive occupants into the possession of the late proprietor, Mr. E. A. Upson. With a natural genius for the business, Mr. Upson saw the capabilities of the Rock and that it might be made one of the most attractive places of summer resort in the country.

By a liberal expenditure of money, and by the exercise of great good taste, he succeeded in uniting at Savin Rock, the conveniences and luxuries which are looked for in a first class hotel, with the special attractions of the watering place.

The house has accommodation for about two hundred boarders. A considerable number of its guests are made up of families who spend the summer at the Rock. The table arrangements are admirable. All who visit the house unite in pronouncing this department unexcelled in the country.

It boasts a shooting gallery, billiard tables, bowling alleys, shuffle board, rowing, sailing, fishing, bathing, double and single carriages, saddle horses, etc., a pleasant and agreeable variety of resources both for the regular guests and for occasional visitors. A dock for the convenient landing of sailing parties has recently been built within a hundred feet of the House.

The house has recently passed into the hands of Harvey Reamer, Esq., of Derby. His charges are three dollars and a half per day.

The facilities for reaching Savin Rock are unusually good. The New York and New Haven Railroad passes within no great distance from the house, the car stopping four times a day at the West Haven Depot. An Omnibus leaves New Haven at 10 a.m. and 2 p.m., and Savin Rock at 11 a.m. and 5:30 p.m. A telegraph office connects the house with all parts of the country. The grounds pertaining to the house embrace about twenty acres, including one of the finest kitchen gardens in the state. The grove continues to be a favorite resort for select picnic parties, a trifling charge being usually made for the use of the grounds and tables.

The pleasant village of West Haven is about a mile distant, having a Congregational and an Episcopal Church, in both of which, visitors to the Rock are received with attention.

In 1860 a serious fire destroyed much of the hotel. It was rebuilt and in 1864 two steam captains, Charles E. Denslow of the "Elm City" and William T. Smith of "The Continental" took over. On September 13, 1870, fire struck the hotel once more, and it was never to be rebuilt.

The following is from the New Haven Palladium, Wednesday, September 14, 1870, describing the fire:

About 4 o'clock on Tuesday morning an alarm of fire was sounded from Box 16, corner of Howard Avenue and Columbus Street. The fire department rallied promptly, but before going far toward the bright light that attracted their attention, it was discovered that the fire was beyond the city limits and somewhere in the vicinity of West Haven. Early in the morning it was ascertained that the Savin Rock House, with most of its attachments and appurtenances, had been destroyed by the devouring element.

What was once the resort of tourists as summer boarders was nothing but a heap of smoldering ruins, the entire structure, excepting the ten-pin bowling alley and the barn across the street, having been consumed.

When the fire was discovered, it was under such headway that it was found impossible to save the building and many of the rooms were filled with smoke; the inmates barely had any time to escape with their lives, many of them rushing out with no other covering than their nightclothes.

Some of the furniture of the lower floors was saved, but the boarders lost most of their clothing. Mr. Gilpin and family were the heaviest losers, almost their entire wardrobe being destroyed. It was fortunate that there was but little breeze at the time, for if there had been, the large barn connected with the hotel would have been destroyed.

The property was formerly owned by Harvey Reamer of Derby but was sold by him to J. H. and T. H. Dawe one year ago last April. The owners estimate their loss at about $30,000.

Most of the boarders, with the owners, transferred themselves to the Sea View House temporarily. Thus has one of our oldest seaside resorts been swept away much to the regret of those who have desired a quiet resort during the warm days of summer.

The origin of the fire has not been distinctly fixed. It is quite evident, however, that it had its origin somewhere in the rear of the building in the vicinity of the laundry and the general impression prevails that it was the work of an incendiary. If so, we hope the parties who committed the crime will be speedily brought to justice.

After the burning of the Savin Rock House, a note of thanks, signed by guests of The Savin Rock House, was unanimously tendered to the Superintendent of the New Haven, West Haven Horse Railroad for his prompt assistance in sending a special car at 4:30 a.m. and removing the guests of the house and their trunks to comfortable quarters free of charge. Also to Mr. Russell of the Sea View House who was promptly on the grounds and tendered us the accommodation of his house, which had been closed for the season. The tender has gladly accepted and Mr. Russell is exerting himself to make us comfortable.

THE FIRST ENTREPRENEURS

George R. Kelsey was Savin Rock's first and greatest entrepreneur and is referred to as the acknowledged father of Savin Rock. Born on May 15, 1820 in Cromwell, Connecticut, he moved with his father to Ohio at age four. There his father and brothers cleared off many acres of heavy timber. George remained with his parents until coming of age, during which time he learned the carpenters' and joiners' trade.

In 1842 he returned to Middletown and soon thereafter his attention was called to the demand for clothing and suspender buckles, which were all imported, and he began in a small way to manufacture these articles.

Possessing but little capital and doing the work by hand, he struggled with persistent energy for ten years to establish the business, struggling the while against terrific foreign competition, and having been burned out twice during that time.

He became president of the Waterbury Buckle Company in 1855, and soon afterward became general manager of the West Haven Buckle Company, holding his interest in both companies up to the time of his death in 1889. He built up a large business for the West Haven Company. Within 27 years under his tenure, $450,000 in dividends was paid to stockholders on a capital investment of $14,000.

Col. Kelsey, who was head of the sixth regiment, Connecticut Volunteers in the Civil War, represented Orange in the General Assembly in 1858, and was successively Town Agent and First Selectman for years. Instrumental in organizing and inaugurating the horsecar lines between New Haven and West Haven, Col. Kelsey, in his desire to be a success, purchased Savin Rock and a portion of its surroundings.

In 1870 he built the Sea View Hotel, partly as a business and partly to boost the wavering horsecar project.

When the Sea View was first erected, it consisted of only the wing facing Beach Street. The Grove Street wing and tower were added years later. Surrounding the hotel were beautiful gardens and lawns. There was but one structure on the waterside for many years, that being a stand conducted by the Orange House. Beautiful flowers bounded every walk, and rose bushes formed semi-secret nooks in which the younger folk delighted to retreat.

Spacious verandas almost surrounding the hotel afforded comfort and opportunity to view the surrounding water and countryside.

From the start it proved to be very popular, and for twenty years or more it was the center of attraction for the elite and aristocratic citizenry of New Haven and surrounding towns.

The hotel was large enough to accommodate 150 guests and became so popular in time that it was impossible to secure a room there unless reservations were made several days in advance. Wealthy people from upstate maintained suites there for seasons, and it was a signal mark of standing to be registered at the "Sea View."

In that same year, George Kelsey built a long pier at the foot of Summer Street which extended out into the harbor for 1,500 feet with a lovely Victorian ice cream parlor jutting off the east side about half way out. Old-fashioned side-wheel excursion steamers would ply between New Haven and Savin Rock, it being considered a delightful experience to sail down the harbor to Kelsey's pier and spend the day there and then return. The steamers "George R. Kelsey", "Pastime" and "Kismet" were all sailed down to the coast of Florida years later by George Kelsey and put to service on the Indian River. His further endeavors included a bandstand, fountain, and an observatory, complete with telescopes for viewing Long Island Sound.

In 1873 George Kelsey gave a huge reception for the Town of West Haven, and an old newspaper clipping is authority for the statement that it was the largest gathering ever recorded at that time. Hundreds of people from New Haven and West Haven attended during the day and night, a band gave music, with dancing going on at both the Sea View and Grove Palace.

Richard Dyer, proprietor of the Elliott House, New Haven, was then manager of the hotel, and with George Kelsey, greeted every visitor and made him or her feel at home. That evening one of the greatest dinners ever served in the town was the culminating event of the day.

The great public reception, as it was called, was followed a few weeks later by a huge canoe race, in which canoeists from Maine to Virginia took part. A pair of Maine woodsmen won the race.

George Kelsey became well-known because of his habit of greeting everyone who came to the Sea View personally and of superintending all of the various functions at the shore. He was a great executive and a man of captivating personality and it has been said of him that he drew people to the shore by sheer friendliness and personality. Scores of campers came to Savin Rock and for these George Kelsey could not do enough. He is spoken of several times in newspaper clippings as "a man whose handshake is a handshake wishing one a genuine welcome."

Being a patriotic man, George Kelsey always planned and successfully carried through, very patriotic Fourth of July celebrations. Several times during the zenith of his career as a hotel proprietor, he gave West Haven gala Fourths due to his executive ability and wide acquaintanceship.

Although the Sea View Hotel had a number of proprietors through the years, the land on which it stood and surrounding property has always been in the possession of the Kelsey and Cameron families. The complete list of proprietors is not known but a fairly accurate one gives Richard Dyer as the first one. Samuel Crane, who was in turn followed by Bodeen and McCarthy, succeeded him. Then came Freeman and Herman Speh. George Cameron was the last proprietor, purchasing the property in 1900 at a cost of $27,000, and he ran the hotel successfully until his death, at which time the trustees of the estate, James T. Copeling and Cornelius A. O'Connell took charge.

In 1922 Judge Gilson of the Probate Court ordered that the still structurally sound old hotel be razed to accelerate the final settlement of the Cameron estate.

Kelsey Avenue was named in George Kelsey's honor.

George R. Kelsey
William Levere's Collection

The Sea View Hotel at the northwest corner of Beach and Grove Streets before the East Wing and Tower were added. circa 1870.

The Sea View Hotel after the addition of the East Wing and Tower. circa 1878.

Looking west down Beach Street along the old horsecar trolley tracks about 1881 with the Sea View Hotel shown at right.

The building of Kelsey's 1,500 ft. pier, off Beach Street, east of Summer Street, 1870.

The Bandstand built by George Kelsey, Savin Rock Park. 1910 photo.

The Fountain built by George Kelsey in 1870. Hotel Ihne in background.

Atop Savin Rock Proper, the Savin Rock Observatory was built by George Kelsey in 1870. The Observatory was destroyed by fire in 1897.

Taylor's Patent Inclined Railway, One of the earliest rides in the Upper Grove. 1872.

The Inclined Railway was a type of Mill Chute without water.

Frank Wilcox

Skeele's Restaurant and Bathing Pavilion during the late 1800's.

Frank Wilcox ranks very high in a select group of Savin Rock entrepreneurs. Area born in 1849, he was educated in local schools. He then served an apprenticeship in the blacksmith trade. He also became Tax Collector for the Town of Orange.

During the late 1800's, a man named Skeele opened a combination restaurant and bathhouse bearing his name. Erected on Beach Street opposite Summer Street, it was very popular for a number of years. One of its features was a subterranean corridor from the area of the kitchen to Kelsey's Pier where seafood was brought in by boats. House specialties included clam chowder and roast clams. Their popularity gave rise to the slogan "The Lights Never Dim at Skeele's.

Frank Wilcox purchased the business in 1900. Within a few years he had withdrawn interest in the bathing pavilion part of the business and concentrated his efforts in greatly enlarging the restaurant until it became known as one of New England's better dining places famous for its fifty and seventy-five cent shore dinners. Being built on pilings over the water, its many windows offered unsurpassed vistas of Long Island Sound from all tables. The old part of the building was made into a penny arcade where those waiting to be served could while away the time.

Installed in the restaurant in 1931 were the first photoelectric self-opening doors between the kitchen and dining area. These were the first in America and four of them were purchased at a cost of $100 each.

Also acquiring Kelsey's Pier, he built the Glee Boat self-sailor ride which had small boats suspended by cables that swung out over the water to the delight of the small fry. Frank Wilcox had previously run the Venetian Swings, Flying Horses, a movie theater and Custer Car ride. Other amusements included a miniature train ride across the street from his restaurant, and a roller-skating rink.

When Wilcox died in 1928, his son-in-law, Frank Terrell, took over and ran the business until 1954 when it was turned into a dance hall.

In 1955 when the Federal, State and City Governments collaborated in pumping sand from the bottom of the Sound to most of the shorefront of West Haven, the property became the "Surf Club" which had cabanas on the beach. After the redevelopment of the mid-1960's when the amusement park was razed, it became city property and was declared a public beach. Wilcox's name was perpetuated in the naming of a steel and concrete pier in the immediate area of his famous restaurant.

Wilcox's Custer Car ride just West of his Roller-Skating Rink.

Wilcox's Glee Boat Self Sailer.

Wilcox's Pier Horses.

Wilcox's Movie Theater.

Wilcox's 175ft. long Dining Room out over the waters of Long Island Sound, 1922.

The first electric trolley on its way to Savin Rock - summer of 1892.

SAVIN ROCK AND THE ELECTRIC TROLLEY

The trolley cars were of great significance relative to Savin Rock. In the days before automobiles became commonplace, Savin Rock and the trolley were dependent on each other for a major part of the prosperity that each enjoyed. Savin Rock needed the tremendous number of people the trolleys brought to them and the trolley company needed the money generated by the thousands of fares collected bringing the fun-seekers to the Rock.

Excerpts from a New Haven newspaper article about 65 years ago follows:

> The first electric trolley car made its debut here on the afternoon of July 16, 1892 and ran from the Central Green in New Haven to Savin Rock. Making the historical run was pioneer motorman, Harry Elmer, while Samuel Hitchcock upheld the dignified position of conductor. The car itself was a crude affair and really was nothing more than one of the single truck horsecars converted into an electric as a result of the installation of a single motor, good old-fashioned air brakes and a variety of crude mechanical and electrical equipment. Remarkable was this first run from the Green to Savin Rock, in that the trip took exactly 30 minutes and a horsecar ride required a full two hours.

> The first electric was the property of the Winchester Avenue Railroad Company of which Israel A. Kelsey was general manager. The company controlled about fifty horsecars and was doing a profitable business when they inaugurated the electrics following the success of the plan in several other New England cities. For some time, no new electrics were purchased by the concern but they converted their old horse drawn cars with motors and all the electrical devices in vogue at that time.

The first electric cars were devoid of any vestibule for the motorman or conductor to stand in. The motorman had to face the severe wintry winds and storms without the slightest protection. During winter storms motormen had to get out and shovel the track for some distance in front of the car or chop off pieces of ice that had frozen to their clothing. There were no stools for the motormen to sit upon and the brakes, which were all crude hand brakes, required a man's strength to operate. Considering all these obstacles, there were few accidents and mishaps.

On the way to Savin Rock. Ward's Corner (Campbell & Elm), ca 1920. Young girl is Anna (Walker) Reilly.

**Albert E. Pond
General Manager of the
Winchester Avenue Street
Railroad.**

Savin Rock
T903

Electric Trolley Car at Savin Rock. Frank Hartshorn, Conductor.

**Connecticut Company "Loop," 1890-1948.
Next to the "Old Ball Park" (where "White City" opened in 1903). People featured are Telco personnel.**

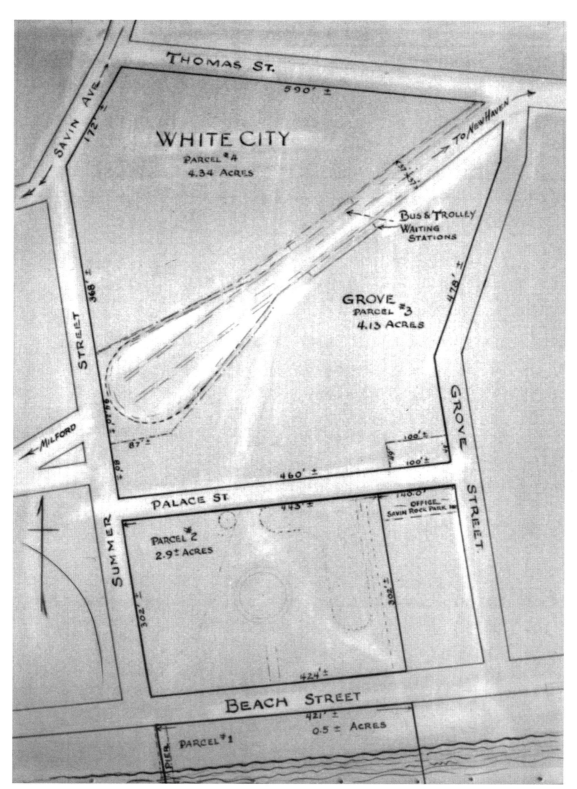

Early map of central portion of Savin Rock.

The Barnacle Restaurant, Bradley Point, Savin Rock.

The Barnacle was set on the southernmost promontory of what today is Bradley Point Park. It was, in the beginning, a tearoom run by a Mrs. Dashiell famous for her four o'clock tea servings. A few additions were made to the structure and a guest house was built. After Mrs. Dashiell's demise, it was taken over by Arthur Wiley who ran it as a seasonal restaurant which became famous for its seafood specialties and spectacular water views. It attracted many notables including author Thornton Wilder who resided in Hamden at one time. Surviving the 1938 hurricane, the restaurant continued to serve guests well into the 1950's when it then became the Wiley's private home until bowing to the redevelopment project in the 1960's.

The Guest House

SPERRY LIGHT

Originally known as the New Haven Outer Breakwall Light, it appeared to be situated at the eastern end of the most westerly breakwater as one gazed out from Savin Rock's shore. However, as one travels westward along the shoreline, it becomes apparent that the west breakwater was constructed northwest to southeast rather than east to west like the other two.

Also, we learn from an accredited authority and historian, Robert G. Bachand's 1989 book, Northeast Lights, that the light preceded the west breakwater by at least fifteen years. The light was operational in January of 1900 while the breakwater wasn't completed until 1915.

Mr. Bachand narrates the many structural problems of erecting and maintaining the light, due to the seven feet of sticky clay at the floor of the sound at that particular area which provided less than stable footing. In 1912 it was officially renamed New Haven Light.

1924 saw the installation of a ten inch air whistle fog signal which gave off a 2 second blast with an interval of 18 seconds, replacing both a 1900 compressed air siren and its 1903 successor, a blower siren.

However, the 61 feet above sea level light was discontinued in 1933, when it was torn down and replaced with a skeleton tower.

Mr. Bachand tells us that, despite its proper name, the old light was almost always referred to as Sperry Light, named for Congressman Nehemiah Sperry, through whose efforts many improvements were made in New Haven Harbor.

Sperry Light, ca 1917. Original photo designated man at rear with pipe as the lighthouse keeper and the boy in front at right center as Irv Batter and at Erv's left, Frank Mullen.

The Adler Cottage was located on Beach Street between Washington and Peck Avenues, 1919. Adler was a partner in the world famous Strouse-Adler Corset Company of New Haven.

Savin Rock "Grove Palace," Upper Grove", a.k.a. "The Park." circa 1880's.

Walter N. Scranton was West Haven's only mounted Patrolman. He patroled Savin Rock from 1904 to 1912.
(Some claim 1905-1910).

Brown's Beach House, opposite Upper Grove, circa 1907.

Photo of a "Beautiful Baby" contest held in the Upper Grove on August 21, 1901. The winner was baby Mildred Otto of Seymour, Connecticut.

The Roller Boller Coaster, located at Hill Street and Campbell Avenue. early 1900's.

Savin Rock Ice Cream and Home Bakery, located at 124 Peck Avenue. George Riehl, Baker. circa 1915.

Putnam's Shore Dinners, early 1900's. Located about opposite Grove Street.

Jack's Grove Hotel, located on Palace at Summer Street in Upper Grove, early 1900's. (Became Carroll's).

The Ferris Wheel, Lower Grove, Savin Rock. circa 1904.

Dr. E. R. Johnson took over the "Keeley Cure" building. This painting of him in 1916 was done by artist Al Reese, who worked at Savin Rock.

Dr. John Anderson was heir to a large tobacco fortune. He sold his home, (*below*) complete with it's own pier and bath houses, to Dr. Keeley of New York, after tax disputes with the town. Then known far and wide as the home of "Keeley's Cure" for alcoholics and drug abusers, it later became The Breakers Convalescent Hospital and the porches were stripped. Still later the tower was removed. It is now known as the "Sandcastle Condominiums." Dr. Anderson also had a large home on Whitney Avenue, New Haven and, at one time, another one on the Thimble Islands off Branford.

Dr. John Anderson home on the northeast corner of Beach Street and Peck Avenue, 1901.

MAYNARD, ARCHITECT.   JAMES O'LOUGHLIN, B

The New Theatre at Savin Rock Park.

An Architect's drawing of the Savin Rock Theater which opened in 1902.

The Savin Rock Theater failed and in 1906, became Bishop's Colonnade.

Yale D. Bishop, owner of Bishop's Colonnade.

Bishop's Colonnade. This photo seemingly depicting a dramatic curve on Beach Street was the result of photographic innovation as the curve was, in actuality, nonexistent.

Russ Levere's Collection

Oriental Park

Oriental Park was a square block bounded by Thomas Street, Peck Avenue, Park Street and East Avenue. The Oriental Park Beach Pavilion was on the waterside at the foot of Peck Avenue and had both bath lockers and an upstairs combination hall and dining area with many windows for water viewing. All families living in the "Park" shared a common yard without fences which was an everyday gathering place for children living in the area. From this very same spot, the chatter and laughter of children is still being heard as they alight from school buses before entering the Savin Rock Community School built on the former Oriental Park grounds.

Mr. and Mrs. Charles Levere in front of their summer home on Park Street Oriental Park site. circa 1903.

In the 1940's, the O'Connell Road House became the Sippican House which eventuated into Savin Rock's first nightclub to feature female impersonators. The Club ran successfully until redevelopment in the 1960's.

The O'Connell Road House, circa 1870, was located on the northeast corner of Beach and Rock Streets.

In "The Park," a.k.a. "Upper Grove" circa 1902.
The Savin Rock Theater can be seen in the background on Beach Street extending out over the water.
Family carriages rolled on dirt roads. In 1906, it became Yale Bishop's Colonnade for fine dining.

The Racer, 1900's. North side of Palace Street.

Riding the Racer, Savin Rock, 1915.

Savin Rock Amusement Park, 1908   T S Bronson

Wilcox's Pavilion and Carousel, 1908. Located on Beach Street at the head of Summer Street.

Looking East on Beach Street in front of Upper Grove (The Park), 1910.

Wilcox's Pier Restaurant, 1910.

Looking East along "Lovers' Lane", 1910.

John St. Lawrence relocated Hill's Homestead here temporarily, while the original building was being renovated, 1910. Beach Street near Peck Avenue.

A group of Excursionists at Miller's Casino, Beach Street, about opposite Grove Street, 1910.

The Somerset Hotel, Bradley Point, 1911. Proprietor Bill Carroll and his wife at center. The Somerset Hotel burned on April 13, 1918.

William H. Brown's Beach House was located on Beach Street just east of the Sea View Hotel. Later on it became Moegling's. circa 1910.

Shoot-the-Chutes with the electric Tower in background. The bridge was destroyed by fire in 1912. It was rebuilt with an arched bridge.

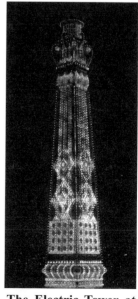

White City, north of the Trolley right-of-way, was opened in 1903 by the Seaside Construction Company. A "Doc" DeWaltoff had a hand in its development (and other areas of the Rock as well). Among its several focal points were the triple arched, 25 foot high main gateway alongside the trolley tracks, the Electric Tower with its hundreds of colored light bulbs situated west of the pear-shaped pond which received boats from the Shoot-the-Chutes, and the White City Flyer, a roller coaster. Included among the many other attractions were the Airdrome, Orpheum, Mitchell's and Clifford's Theaters. Just inside the main gateway was a carousel, a bandstand, the "Bay State Limited" miniature train, Giant Swing, a dance hall and a restaurant. Fireworks were a regular feature as were balloon ascensions with parachute drops. Daredevils of the day included one who rode a bicycle down the incline of the Chutes and at the bottom vaulted over the handlebars into the pond. Another, while performing a slide down a guy-wire attached to the Electric Tower and holding onto a mouthpiece by his teeth, lost his grip and fell to his death. In the early 1920s vandals used ropes to pull down the beautiful Tower.

The Electric Tower at night.

White City Entrance, 1911. A beautiful entrance to an enchanting amusement area.

Circle Swing, just inside and a bit west of Main Entrance to White City. circa 1908.

The Shoot-the-Chutes showing the rebuilt arched bridge.

A postcard of the Shoot-the-Chutes pool in White City, 1920.

Murphy's (later Giuliano's) Carousel Organ. Beach Street, Savin Rock.

White City's first carousel and train ride.

White City Entrance during Mardi Gras, 1912.

White's Trained Animal Show, Mardi Gras, 1911.

Souvenir Stand on Beach Street, Circa 1912.

Corey's Ice Crean Parlor located on Grove Street, during Mardi Gras, 1912.

Mardi Gras, Beach Street, 1911 or 1912.

Mitchell's Theater, White City, Savin Rock. circa 1911.

Clifford's Theater, White City, Savin Rock.

Grove Lunch, Railroad Grove near Old Mill. circa 1911

Roller Skating Rink, Campbell Avenue and Beach Street, the future site of the Virginia Reel.

The Waiting Station at Savin Rock with Old Mill in background, 1911.

"Scenic Railway" White City area, Savin Rock, early 1900's.

THE KICKAPO INDIAN Medicine Show around the turn of the century always attracted crowds at Savin Rock. Intermingled with the entertainment was the selling of medicine made in New Haven, "guaranteed to cure any ailment from A to Z."

The Kickapoo Indian Medicine Show, at Savin Rock, Lower Grove, 1910.

This horse was a part of a sideshow at Savin Rock during the 1920's and could, supposedly, give correct addition answers by tapping his front hoof.

Harrigan's "Lilliputian" Theater, Savin Rock Grove, 1895.

"Palm Reading" in 1906, Lower Grove area of Savin Rock. Hope Ives and Doc Edwards are seated at the right.

Postcard showing "Auto Row" on Beach Street. Bishop's Colonnade on the right, 1920's. A Mr. Brennan charged motorists a fee to park on the street. He was eventually forced to "cease and desist."

Bishop's Colonnade at night. circa 1912.

William Levere's Collection

John Cox's Surf House built a short time after the end of the Civil War was famous for steaks, chicken and shore dinners. circa 1890.

The Shingle Hill auto and motorcycle races were held in 1910, 1911 and 1912. A few comments from Harold Hornstein's 1972 article is included in the following:

After meeting at Automobile Headquarters (Cox's) at Savin Rock, the participants proceeded on to Lake Phipps and readied to start the grueling race up the steep climb of Shingle Hill Road. The auto races began at the Lake, then up the hill to the finish line at the water tower. Amid clouds of dust and oil smoke, with fire emerging from their exhaust pipes, they huffed and puffed their way up the steep dirt road to the finish line. It was a true test for cars of yesteryear - their ability to climb a steep hill in high gear. A much talked about event occurred when one of the cars threw a wheel halfway up and went out of commission, but the wheel kept on going and actually made it to the top! Competition included some famous names that were to go down in the history of car racing. Spectators were treated to the unforgettable antics of Barney Oldfield, with his big cigar and his cap on backwards, who took his Blitzen Benz up in record-breaking time.

Cox's Inn - "Automobile Headquarters." Cars met here before and after the hill-climbing races on nearby Shingle Hill at Lake Phipps. Popular for many years until a roadway connecting Ocean Avenue and Beach Street on the southern side of Savin Rock Proper was blasted into the rocky crag. The concussion of each blast caused much cosmetic damage and let dirt encroach inside the once lovely Inn. This, coming on top of the banning of liquor in the 1920's during the prohibition era, proved fatal to the old Inn and it was closed permanently.

Cox's, 1921 - 1922.

Russ Levere's Collection

**Shingle Hill Climbing Race
1911**

C. R. Robinson - S.P.O.

C. S. Bragg - National.

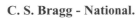

C. D. Brainard - Carreja.

C. Lee - Cutting.

E. C. Bull - Buick.

H. Boner - Oakland.

Baseball Grounds, Home Field of the New Haven Colonial League Team, Savin Rock in 1912.
The first game of the season.

On a triangular parcel of land bounded by Oak and Marsh Streets and Savin Avenue is where the old ballpark from the White City site had been moved. By then, New Haven's team played in the Colonial League and they became champions of the 1912 season with such luminaries as "Pop" Foster, Johnny Nagle and West Haven's one and only "Moose" Miller. The stands were entered from Marsh Street, near Morgan. In the mid-twenties, the creaky old stands were razed and a new era evolved. George Weiss (who later became General Manager of the New York Yankees) owned the New Haven franchise in the Eastern League. He had been operating out of a ballpark named for him in Hamden, Connecticut on a plot of land bounded by Woodin, Murray, Helen and Notkins Streets, which was about to be redeveloped. The Weiss Park stands were moved to West Haven, with the stands radiating west and south from the corner of Savin And Oak. It was renamed Donovan Field after the late manager, "Wild Bill" Donovan, an ex-big league pitcher, who switched bunks with George Weiss just before the train they were on was involved in a wreck where Donovan was killed. A bronze marker serving as a monument was placed in center field. Upon demolition, it was presented to George Weiss at Yankee Stadium where it will remain as part of a collection of memorabilia.

Donovan Field, early on, was the scene of West Haven High School football, Police Field Days and some boxing. After the demise of the Eastern League during the Great Depression, local fans began to take note of a Harry Noyes-Moe Quigley semi-pro team that had played some games there. By the time World War II began, the West Haven Sailors were a smooth, power-packed team with the likes of Ed "Bird Dog" Hennessey, Joe Binkoski, George "Ginger" Klivak, Bill Doherty, Johnny White, Joe Rossamondo, Jack McWeeney and "Shorty" Torello, among others. During the War, they were bolstered by big leaguers Cy Block, Jim Gleason, Billy Johnson, Jim Bagby and a chubby pitcher who used the name Davis. Some great rivalries were kindled during that period, especially with the Arma Club from Long Island.

To anyone not of that era, it may sound heretical to proclaim the biggest drawing card of all to have been an umpire but, during those war years, it was so. When Al Barlick, who later became Umpire-in-Chief in the National League, called out "STE-R-R-RIKE" in his booming voice and well-orchestrated body postures, it never failed to fire up the crowd. While Barlick received the loudest cheers, his partner on the bases, "Pop" O'Neil had to endure a thunderous chorus of "Boos" whenever he made a decision. They were affectionate "Boos" though, for "Pop" had been around for years and was very well liked.

Entering the ballpark, you could depend on a personal greeting from the always genial Billy French, while Earl Strong's booth atop the stands would be blaring out popular songs of the day with "Pistol Packin' Mama" played so often it became the unofficial theme song of the fans. If you didn't run into "Shrimp" Flynn (who always had a definite opinion on any subject) you'd be sure to bump into "Moose" Miller who could (and did) tell you about baseball in the "Good Old Days."

The great Babe Ruth played at Donovan Field in an exhibition game. There were no unfilled seats that day and those lucky enough to be in attendance left remarking on the love that radiated between "The Babe" and the fans. It was a day to be added to the "Savin Rock Days to be Remembered" list.

Looking west along first base stands at a Donovan Field Eastern League game. circa 1935.

West Haven Sailors home game at Donovan Field during the WW II era.

61

In the early 1930's, a racetrack was added and Harry Ryan introduced midget auto racing here with such favorites as Ron Householder, "Wild Bill" Holmes, Bill Schindler (who continued to race and win after losing a leg in an accident) and Bridgeport's "Pickles" Bicklehaupt. After the midget craze subsided, Harvey Tattersall entered the picture with stock car racing. A local lad named Billy Greco immediately became the favorite of the fans with superlative driving. Donovan Field, while it never lost its identity completely, had become known as the West Haven Speedway.

Donovan Field Police Field Day. circa 1938.

Donovan Field Police Field Day. circa 1940.

The New Haven Baseball Team, Connecticut League, 1908. Owner George
Cameron in the center.

Don Cameron's Collection

The 1912 Champs of the Connecticut League.
New Haven Baseball Club, Connecticut League, 1912.

Top row: Bill Hopper; Harry Fanwell; Jerry Connell; Moose Miller; E. "Slim"
Foster; Bill Jensen; Carl Flick; Kid Sherwood.
Bottom row: Joe Pepe; Clyde Waters; "Bugs" Reisigl; C. Pop Foster; Irwin
Gough; Johnnie Nagle; Fred Daschbach.

Both teams played in the old Savin Avenue ball park that was razed in the 1920's
to make way for what became known as Donovan Field.

The West Haven Sailors.

This picture was taken at Quigleys Grandstand Restaurant located at the corner of Savin Avenue and Noble Street, West Haven, Connecticut, in 1935.

Left to right, top row: Maurice Quigley; Jack McSherry.

Second row: George Albinger; Ray Hartmann; Paul Massey; John McHugh; Marty Trotsky; Jim Matthews; George Heyer.

First row: Hap Sutphin; Beans Torcellini; Joe Lawson; Jack Lockery; Bill Montagna; Luke Crowe.

Batboy unidentified.

Bill Blatchley

Bill Blatchley was emcee and fight announcer at White City Stadium and other spots. Fans loved to "boo" him, no matter what he said, but he was the most popular of all in his day and a great drawing card at any event. circa 1940.

Vinny Carbone,

Vinny Carbone was West Haven's favorite sportswriter. As a teenager, Vinny had a sports column in the New Haven Register called "Carbone's Corner" and wrote for the Register and West Haven's weekly paper for many years. He was sometimes referred to as "Mr. Jimmy Fund" for his many years of effort for that worthy cause. Vinny loved Savin Rock and it was evident in the articles he wrote on the old Rock in the 1980's.

"Babe" Driscoll, Dillman and Cowles at the White City Stadium, Savin Rock, 1940's.

Looking west on Bradley Avenue, Bradley Point, 1913. This view is from the junction of Bradley and Ocean Avenues. The Columbia Hotel at right was once owned by a Mr. Boardman and was later acquired by Bill Carroll. It burned in 1918.

Back of original said 41 Grove Street. Another old shot shows a grocery store on lower Campbell Avenue with the same name. circa 1919. Grove Street was changed to Altschuler Plaza during redevelopment of the 1970's.

"Girls at the Rock." Woman standing at right is Miss Cushman, a balloonist at Savin Rock. circa 1910.

Balloon ascension at Savin Rock. circa 1910.

Savin Rock Bathhouse, 1914. Lady at right was Helen Nix Stokes, mother of Mary Stokes Ahern.

NEW HAVEN'S HARBOR'S THREE BREAKWATERS

A peripheral part of the Savin Rock mystique stands staunchly out in the sound -- New Haven harbor's three breakwaters. Taken for granted by most, they are, nevertheless, the focus of the eyes of those who look seaward from the beach areas, piers and at one time from the first dip on the old Thunderbolt roller coaster. A short history of the breakwaters by Frank P. Malinconico as published in the New Haven Register on July 22, 1979 seems apropos at this time and reads as follows:

"For more than a century they've guarded the entrance to New Haven Harbor, welcoming sailors home from the sea. Neither time nor the endless pounding of the surf has changed their faces. Today they stand as a silent reminder of New Haven's past.

For most people, the breakwaters in New Haven Harbor are just another pile of rocks holding back the tide. And except for a few seagulls, no one pays much attention to them. But embedded in each rock is something very special. It is the history of a harbor and its people.

New Haven Harbor was buzzing with excitement during the 1870s. Sloops, schooners and barges jammed the channels. And trading seemed to be getting better every year. According to retired Cap't. Jack Seymour, 'On a given day 100 ships crowded the docks, while 100 others waited at anchor for favorable weather in open water.' This worried Capt. Charles H. Townsend and his friends. Every 10 years severe storms had wiped out the frail vessels anchored in the harbor. The ships needed protection or commerce would be ruined.

In 1873 the construction of breakwaters was urged by such area notables as Yale President Theodore D. Woolsey, Mayor A.B. Bigelow, Townsend and Thomas Trowbridge. The breakwaters would provide ships with a 'harbor of refuge at a midpoint in the sound.' The men were supported by groups from New York to New London. Townsend felt that the breakwaters would encourage more vessels to pass through the harbor. And commerce would improve.

The Harbor and River Act of 1879 approved construction for the eastern and middle breakwaters. The project was assigned to the Army Corps of Engineers in Providence, R.I. (In 1948 the corps became a single bureau in Waltham, Mass.) Construction began in 1880 on a dike jutting out from Sandy Hook. Rock taken from the channel entrance was used to build the eastern breakwater. By 1894 both eastern and middle breakwaters were completed. But it still was not enough.

Southwesterly storms continued to damage unprotected ships anchored in the harbor. A third breakwater was constructed on the western side of the harbor in 1904. The entire project was officially completed in 1915 at a cost of $1,242,246.

Each of the three riprap breakwaters is 10 football fields long and 12 feet high.

According to Walter Mackie of the Army Corps of Engineers in Waltham, Mass., each slab of granite is 3 feet thick and weighs about 2 tons. He added that a million and a half tons of granite were used to build the three breakwaters.

The granite was probably taken from quarries in the Stony Creek area. John Brainerd, a Branford resident, remembers the quarries. 'The stone used for the breakwaters was not adaptable for monumental use. It was uncut and unpolished stone,' he said. 'There were several big quarries around Stony Creek. But Beady's and the Brooklyn Quarry were probably the biggest suppliers. In the early stages of construction, stones were ferried out to the sound by Schooner. Later, barges or tugboats were used. The stones were loaded on the barges and taken to the site. On the sound, laborers would lower the huge slabs into the 30 feet of water by A-frame hoists. 'There were plenty of immigrants who worked on the breakwaters,' notes Brainerd. 'Scots, Swedes and Irish immigrants worked on the quarries. Most of the masons were Italians or Cornishmen from England.'

The breakwaters are not held together by mortar or cement. But according to Mackie they're built to withstand wave action and severe storms. 'We usually overdesign by 10 per cent to reduce the need for costly inspections,' he said. 'But when the breakwater becomes eroded or ruptured, it must be repaired immediately,' he added. 'Ruptures rarely occur, but sometimes a large ship or a record-breaking storm may damage the breakwaters.'

One thing that has changed since 1915 is the cost of building them. It would cost an estimated $40 million to build the breakwaters today.

As for the entire harbor, a lot of changes have been made since Townsend's days. The vast waterway that once extended to the Green has been filled in over the years. And today Townsend would have a tough time crossing Long Wharf by boat. 'It's true,' agrees Gaddis Smith, Yale professor, and harbor historian. 'At one time, most of New Haven was under water. The first settlers probably landed at the corner of George and College Streets. In fact, when workers were digging the foundation for Lee High School, they found huge stone pilings from a seawall.'

So the next time you're driving near Long Wharf, think about that pile of rocks in the Sound. There's a lot more to those breakwaters than meets the eye."

About 1948, Jack Lynch, West Haven's Town Engineer at that time, stated to this scribe that, in his opinion, if there had been no breakwaters during the hurricane of Sept. 21, 1938, Savin Rock would probably have been a total loss.

E. F. Raffile's Restaurant in 1920, located on the corner of Palace and Grove Streets.

This coaster from Raffile's Palace Cafe reads: "May our faults be written on the seashore, and every good action prove a wave to wash them out."

Stanford's Hotel was located on the northeast corner of Beach and Morgan Streets. The last building on this site was a roller skating rink, supplanted by an Arcade which burned in the 1960's.

The Sea View Hotel, northwest corner of Beach and Grove Streets. Built for George Kelsey in 1870, it was owned by the Cameron family at the time of this late teens photo and was razed in the early 1920's.

A group of motorcyclists at the Rock, Beach Street near Summer Street, 1910.

Motor Drome, at Savin Rock was very popular for a time. circa 1920.

Postcard of The Orpheum Theater, White City.

The Orpheum Theater was one of many theaters (though perhaps the best remembered) that sprang up in the triangular area named White City. This one was victim of a 1921 fire that totally destroyed it. In its place there evolved a boxing and wrestling arena named White City Stadium, which regularly drew capacity crowds during the summer season. It presented both amateur and professional bouts and catered to a surprising number of fans of the so-called weaker sex.

This postcard gives a view of the theater from the stage. The seating capacity on this card states 2000, while others give both 1000 and1500.

The cast of a local revue at the Orpheum Theater at White City, Savin Rock on December 29, 30 and 31 in 1916.

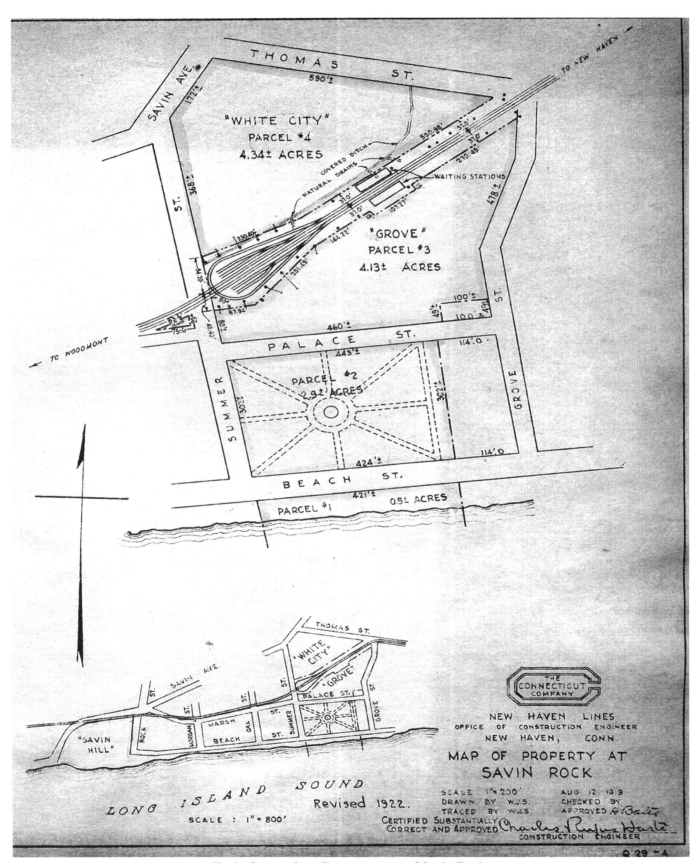

Early Connecticut Company map of Savin Rock.

Most historians agree on 1871 as the year Charles Hagar ran the first carousel at Savin Rock. It was a portable affair, moved from place to place by horsecart and propelled by human muscle attached to a rope. A few years later, after Julius Lambert acquired it, a horse did the pulling. Years later after electrification, Lynch operated flying horses here.

Lambert's Carousel, 1921.

Lynch's Carousel, 1922.

Wilcox's Merry-Go-Round, Beach Street, Savin Rock. circa 1924.

Looking South from White City at the trolley right-of-way, 1927.

Tub Races and Madame Annette, Palmist, White City, 1922.

"White Way Lunch," Summer Street opposite Lower Grove, early 1920's.

CHAPTER TWO

~~~~~~~

THE WAY WE REMEMBER

Looking southeast across Savin Rock's main artery, Beach Street. Small building at bottom center was Art Larrivee's store. The large building with octagonal top was Wilcox's rebuilt theater building (after a disastrous conflagration which encompassed most of the entire block). It later housed a skating rink and was used for a 1933 dance marathon. The last amusement it held was Peter Franke's Fun House. Directly across Beach Street was Wilcox's Pier Restaurant. Abutting it's eastern elevation, part of the pier is visible and, just east of that, the Thunderbolt. Near the bottom left is the Mill Chutes. Diagonally upward is the Motorboat Ride with segments of its canal visible and just across the Midway at its left is the famous Hotel Ihne. The wooded area at left-center was part of the Upper Grove (earlier called The Park).

The Devil Roller Coaster was part of Liberty Pier and was levelled by fire with the rest of the pier complex in 1932. It was across the street from Jake's who had the first, and much copied, "charcoal broiled" hot dogs.

Noah's Ark was at Savin Rock from 1925 to 1934 when it burned. North side of Beach Street, between Oak and Summer Streets.

Murphy's Pier. Light House Ferry about 250 yards east of Kelsey/Wilcox's Pier, 1920 -1921.

Kelsey/Wilcox's Pier, 1928. Thunderbolt on left. Glee Boat Self-Sailor on right.

The Zephyr, along with her sister ship, S.S. Cynthia plied Long Island Sound between Savin Rock and Lighthouse Point. circa 1917.

The S.S. Cynthia, landing at Wilcox's Pier. circa 1919.

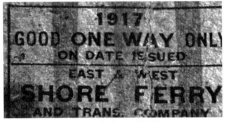

Ferry ticket, 1917.

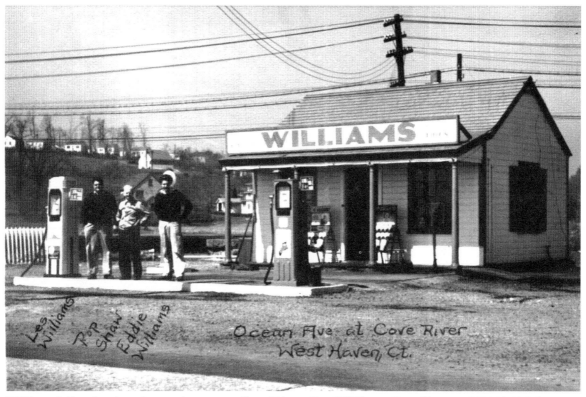

Williams' Gas Station, Ocean Avenue at Cove River. Les Williams, Pop Shaw and Eddie Williams at right, 1940.

Old trolley passing over Cove River at about the westernmost periphery of Savin Rock, about one half mile from the "Trolley Loop" off Summer Street. circa 1920's.

Claude Birchman
A breathing machine to register lung power.

"Pop" Carroll, Tom Young, young Bill Carroll and Tom Wade during prohibition in the 1920's. Pop Carroll was a Savin Rock entrepreneur who was the catalyst behind this photo of the burial of "John Barleycorn - killed by prohibition June 30, 1919." Notice that each of the "mourners" holds a form of libation in his hand and that the grave is bedecked with empty bottles. 'Twas a sad day for many tinder-dry throats.

"Missouri Mules" was located on the South side of Beach Street a bit east of Summer Street. Third from the left is Col. Lewis W. Field.

The Band Stand, Savin Rock, 1923.

Postcard contains error. Grove Street ran parellel to Midway and was on the eastern side of the Hotel Ihne shown here on the left. 1924.

Wilcox's Pier Restaurant employees. circa 1920's.

Yacht in front of Cox's Surf House, just east of Bradley Point, 1923.

Looking toward the Trolley Right-of-Way. The building at right later became the Wax Museum. Lynch's Carousel is visible near left center, 1923.

Billiards owner Lou Romano with Mike Gagliardi, John Gagliardi and Joe Romano. circa 1921.

Bedelia, a paper mache figure with a man on stilts inside, 1920's.

Fred Levere with two Eskimo children who, with their parents were part of one of the many sideshows at White City during the 1900's.

Well-known from the early days of the 20th century in Savin Rock entrepreneurial circles, the Levere's were a driving force in the growth and diversification of the grand old park. Father Fred, a perfect symbol of astuteness during his lifetime at the Rock, sired two sons who became part of the family ventures (many fingers in many pies) that was the sometimes ephemeral business of anticipating the season to season desires of the general public at any amusement park. Son, Ed, became a lawyer, but retained interest in the family business. The other son, Bill, learned all the nuances of the business through active participation and, having learned the craft, loved it and stayed with it. Bill's two sons, Ron and Russ, were both inculcated in Savin Rock lore as young lads but the glorious world of the Rock ended while they were still young.

Both Fred and son Ed have passed on. Bill's son, Ron, teaches up in Maine and Russ is an overseas envoy and troubleshooter for a very large CT corporation.

Ed Levere, 1952.

Bill leads a fairly quiet life but has hosted at his home every Thursday night a group of old "Rock Rats" euphemistically called "Club 90" who eat, drink, are mostly merry and love to reminisce. These evenings have been going on since the closing of the Rock in the mid-sixties. Perhaps this little jingle personifies the ambiance there:

At the table in Bill's kitchen
Where all the goodies dwell
There's lots of talk - no friction
And the "Rock" doth cast its spell
Libations rest within the "box"
Whose door is mostly open
There rests on those a mighty pox
Who merely sit there hopin'
The boys come in and all shake hands
No "high fives" for them
Perhaps someday in Beulah Land
They'll do it all again!

William (Bill) Levere, 1952.

Fred Levere, owner of Park Lunch is shown here with his son Ed in the 1920's.

Park Lunch employees, 1922. Owner Fred Levere at rear in white "Panama" type hat. Man at his left (in cap) is believed to be his son, Ed.

"Murray" is the Ticket Taker during this Sideshow in the 1920's. Bill Levere at right center.

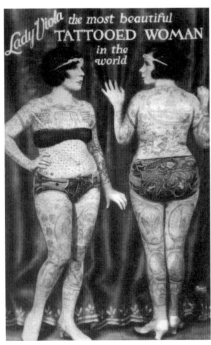

Lady Viola, the most beautiful tattooed woman in the world could be seen at Savin Rock in the early 1900's.

Blinky, billed at a Savin Rock Sideshow as Half Seal/Half Boy in 1927.

Abe Goldstein, 1927.
A friendly and very obliging fellow, was
Savin Rock's favorite clown.

Abe Goldstein with Art Fries of the West
Haven Police Department, 1927.

Savin Rock Sideshow, Upper Grove, 1929.

"Miller" Motor Car for sightseeing, 1918.

One hundred and ten year old Tillie, the
elephant, with trainer Fitzie.
Little girl is Helen Levere, 1927.

Al Nachand, One Man Band, circa 1933.
Al worked for the Levere's until the mid
1960's. He performed there through the
1930's and worked various rides as
ticket taker.

A Camel Ride, White City, near "Lookout Bridge".
The "Arab" in this photo actually came from Italy.

Sideshow, Lower Grove, 1931.

Sideshow, Lower Grove, 1928.

R-5/18/67

The Savin Rock Hose Co. started after an 1888 fire destroyed Hinman's Astor house where Dadd's Hotel was later. Originally called the Seaside Hose Co., located at the northwest corner of Holmes and Hill Streets.

Savin Rock House Co. # 4. Photo taken at the Connecticut State Firemen's Convention, August 19, 1927. Northwest corner of Holmes and Hill Streets.

Standing: 5th from left, Charles Darby; 2nd from right, Vincent Leo.
Seated: 2nd from left, Sylvester Brians; 3rd from right, "Mustard" Carlo.
All others unknown.

Cox's Train located on Beach Street, opposite Wilcox's Pier Restaurant, 1927.

Mill Chutes located on the East side of Summer Street, just South of the Trolley Loop, 1927.

Postcard of the original Thunderbolt, built in 1925.

The Famous Thunderbolt Roller Coaster was built in 1925 by Prior, Church and Traver on a pier supported by spiles out over the water. It was 505 Feet long from the waters edge out into Long Island Sound and was a breathtaking sight to see. Its highest spot was 93 feet from the pier and its main drop was 85 feet of sheer thrilling terror to within 8 feet of the main deck. Wilcox's pier on its western side was almost always crowded by folks too timid to ride the Thunderbolt, but were nonetheless enthralled by watching the more daring riders as they roared up, down and around the curves at breakneck speed while gripping the safety bars, or each other, and letting loose banshee screams of both merriment and fright. Destroyed by the 1938 hurricane, it was rebuilt in 1939 by Ackley, Bradley and Day and renamed "Giant Flyer." The public outcry at the name change soon caused the owners to rename the coaster the "Thunderbolt-Giant Flyer." The new name was never accepted by the public and the ultimate thrill ride at Savin Rock was always referred to as the "Thunderbolt." The coaster was finally razed in 1957 because of rotting spiles on its understructure.

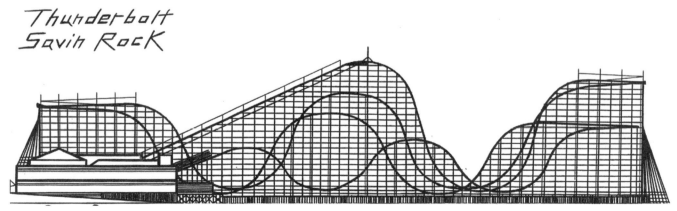

Thunderbolt drawing by Joe Santore.

The entrance to the Thunderbolt. South side of Beach Street, just east of Summer Street, 1938.

Thunderbolt, 1938.

Tryus Lunch. Nobody seems to be sure of its location but best guess is Beach Street east of Campbell Avenue or West of Summer Street. circa late teens.

Located at 35 Grove Street, the Seery House was one of many thirst emporiums on this street at various times, 1928.

Curren's Gas Station.

Photo courtesy of Raymond Curren and Dot Curren Marinan

While servicing a customer, **Bill Curren**
shows his usual pleasant greeting that
helped make his service station # 1 to Savin
Rockers.

Curren and Ready Service Station, # 92 on the old Savin Avenue, had a name change to just Currens shortly after opening when the partnership dissolved and Ready left for greener pastures. It soon became one of the best known service stations in West Haven during the 1920's, 30's and 40's. It's owner, Bill Curren, was a very popular Prospect Beach resident and to state that you were "going to get gas" meant you were taking a trip to Currens. One of the best stories told about "The Thinker" statue sitting upon the station's roof is that the Yale Art School had discarded the statue and a couple of friendly funsters placed it over the doorway of the station during the night as a surprise for its owner. Bill Curren goodnaturedly kept it in its prominent spot for many years enjoying the comments from motorists. It is of interest to note that the houses viewed to the left of Curren's Station were located in the very spot now occupied by Turk's Restaurant located on the newly named Captain Thomas Blvd. And how about the 23 cents per gallon gasoline sign!

The Hotel Ihne was built on Grove Street at the corner of Palace Street in 1907 and rapidly became a favorite of Yalies and more conservative patrons who appreciated the homelike atmosphere and super cleanliness of the 25 room inn. It contained several dining areas, a spotless bar just off the Midway, and a rathskeller. Bill and Ethel Ihne were among the most liked and appreciated of all hosts at Savin Rock. Your author visited there many times in his youth in the company of his Dad, who had played piano there in his younger days, and vividly remembers that the first beer for Dad was always on the House 'In memory of our younger days when we were just starting' or similar language. Such were the Ihnes!

Hotel Ihne, 1921.

Bill and Ethel Ihne, 1931.

Inside the Hotel Ihne, 1916.

The Circus in White City Stadium looking southeast. White City Entrance in background. This is the former site of the Opheum Theater, destroyed by fire in 1921.

White City Motor Boat Ride located at the old Shoot-The-Chutes pond, 1931.

Fred Levere, owner of White City on left, Al Rees, an artist who worked at the Rock is at right, Beach Street, 1936.

"Thru The Orient" on Thomas Street, White City, 1930's.

Pavilion Royale on Beach Street where Worthy Hills, Barney Rapp and Rudy Vallee orchestras were popular in the late 1920's through the mid 1930's. Rapp's brother, Barry Wood, later sang regularly on radio's Lucky Strike Hit Parade.

McEnelly's "Singing Orchestra" held sway during the mid-teens at Jackson's Palais de Danse on Summer Street until a 1917 fire destroyed it along with most of the rest of the block.

Barney Rapp's Orchestra. He went to the midwest after leaving Savin Rock and both Rosemary Clooney and Doris Day give him much credit for the impetus he provided in the early days of their careers.

Marathon Dance Teams in 1933. Left to right: #12 Chas "Pop" Myers & Doris King; #4 "Wiggles" Royce & Dot Hopkins; #27 Jimmie Barrett & Anna Loftus; #11 Al & Ruth Smith; #5 Eddie & Zola Nolan; #10 Frank Lovecchio & Ruth Johnstone. This dance marathon at Wilcox's was won by the couple at the extreme right, Ruth Johnstone and Frank Lovecchio who later went on to fame as singer Frankie Laine.

Dot Hopkins and "Wiggles" Royce, were two very popular dancers at the marathons of the 1930's.

Liberty Pier, Savin Rock, 1922 -1932.

Liberty Pier, a cerebral conception of 1922 which evolved into an enormously popular area of the Rock. It boasted of a fantastic fun house called Bluebeard's Castle, a carousel, frozen custard and refreshment stands and one of Savin Rock's unforgettable thrill rides, "The Devil" roller coaster which some oldsters remember as the fastest ride of them all. Unfortunately, the entire complex went up in flames in 1932. The Stand at left was forerunner of "Nickel Charlie's" in New Haven.

Liberty Pier after the devastating fire in 1932.

All that is left of The Devil roller coaster as firemen pour water over the smoldering rubble, 1932.

View from over Donovan Field/West Haven Speedway looking southeast. The Mill Chutes at the corner of Summer Street and the Trolley "Loop" is shown at upper left. Wilcox's old theater building which was once a skating rink, marathon dance hall and later became Peter Franke's Fun House is shown directly across from Wilcox's Pier Restaurant in the upper right corner. circa 1937.

Trolley "Loop." circa 1930's.

Pep Johnson

"Pep" Johnson was one of the best known of all Savin Rock entrepreneurs, having a nickname that seemed symbolic of the park area. He was the father of Bill Johnson, West Haven's Fire Department Chief who, in turn, sired Bill "Wiggy" Johnson, our present fire chief. Pep's other progeny were Bob, a former Mayor of West Haven, Fred, a well-known local politician and Frank, an entity of note in the mercantile field. A few roving youngsters, including this scribe, always skipped Pep Johnson's stand when out for a few moments of deviltry at the Rock. We learned, early on, that "Pep" could handle quickly and effortlessly any smart-alecky show-offs with ease. We remember him with a chuckle and with respect. circa 1930's.

Matty Coyle, Jr. on the right and (believed to be) Herb Anderson on the left having a go at hockey practice on the frozen over Long Island Sound with Sperry Light as the backdrop, 1934.

WHEN AT SAVIN ROCK
DON'T FORGET
'Pep' Johnson's
Stand

IN THE GROVE - - - SAVIN ROCK

Around the turn of the century, folks started putting up summer homes along what became Bradley Avenue out on the Point. They were a mixture of professional, artistic and mercantile people who appreciated the lovely view of Long Island Sound and the sense of privacy the "off-the-beaten-path" area provided. Years later, when the buildings were being razed, workers and gawkers were surprised to see ornate carved woodwork and other niceties in the interiors of the homes, some of whose outer shells looked a little less elegant.

Fred Farnsworth's Collection

Death Valley Fun House on Beach Street opposite the Upper Grove. The skull and cross-bones lasted only for the 1938 season and was replaced by the "laughing Lady" whose raucous laughter reverberated throughout this section of the Rock.

Frank Mullen was West Haven's first lifeguard in the 1930s and was stationed at the town's only public beach located by Farino's Refreshment Stand on Sea Bluff Beach. This spot was considered the start of a Savin Rock visit by all of his Prospect Beach neighbors as they trekked across the trolley trestle over Cove River or crossed the bridge over the dike leading to Bradley Point. Frank later became a West Haven dentist with offices on Savin Ave. where he could often be found serenading his patients with the song "Life is Just a Bowl of Cherries" while their open mouths awaited his dental work. His assistants all claimed that Frank had accomplished the unbelievable -- he had become a dentist truly loved by his patients.

Draper's Bathing, 1938. Five cents for an all-day swim. Located at the foot of Campbell Avenue with the Virginia Reel in background and Bingo at right center.

A close-up view of Draper's showing diving platform and raft, 1938.

Hurricane damage on Beach Street 9-21-38.

Bradley Point damage from the 1938 hurricane.

Drapers' Bathing, off Beach Street at Campbell Avenue after the 1938 hurricane.

Morse Park area, Beach Street, looking toward Savin Rock, 1938.

Morse Park area of Beach Street after the 1938 hurricane.

The Kiddy Park, Upper Grove alongside Summer Street after the 1938 hurricane.

1938 hurricane damage to the Thunderbolt roller coaster.

Lower Beach Street damage from the hurricane of 1938.

Wilcox's Restaurant after the hurricane of 1938.

Wilcox's Pier and the Thunderbolt after the hurricane of 1938.

A closer look at the hurricane damage to the Thunderbolt.

Lynch's Carousel, Railroad Grove, damaged by the hurricane.

Hurricane damage to White City Archway, 1938.

The Dike at outlet of Cove River. Citizens begin the huge task of cleaning up and rebuilding the area, 1938.

William (Bill) Levere on the catwalk of the Thunderbolt-Giant Flyer, performing the daily inspection, 1940.

The rebuilding of the Thunderbolt as the "Giant Flyer" in 1939.

The workers who helped rebuild the Thunderbolt, pictured here with owner, Fred Levere on the extreme left, 1940.

The Thunderbolt-Giant Flyer, 1940.

Author's Collection

Steve Francis, Ticket Taker for the Thunderbolt-Giant Flyer, 1941.

Harold, George and Earl Hartmann.

Harold Hartmann is a true son of Savin Rock, having been brought up in the peripheral area of the Grand Old Park and still resides in the Sea Bluff section of West Haven which abuts the western perimeter of the old Rock. His earliest memory of the Rock is riding the old Virginia Reel which was run by his father, Raymond.

Starting his maintenance career in the White City area in 1933 as a helper, he was involved in moving Kiddy Rides from White City to "The Park," a.k.a. the "Upper Grove." Hartmann worked his way up the ladder during the thirties serving as operator of various rides, carpenter's helper, brakeman on the Thunderbolt, etc.

In 1940, he became a maintenance man for the rides and during the daytime took a job with the High Standard Co. in Hamden where he eventually became General Plant Superintendent while still doing Savin Rock maintenance work at night and on weekends and holidays.

Enlisting in the Navy in 1942, he served in the Pacific on the U.S.S. Santa Fe, one of the most highly and often decorated ships in the war.

In 1946, after his Navy stint, he returned to both High Standard and Savin Rock. The Levere family, for whom he worked, made him head of the maintenance crew partly because of his genius in fashioning replacement parts for the mechanical parts of the rides, which were, at times, hard to get -- when time was of the essence.

By 1936 brother Earl had started there and in 1953 the youngest brother, George, decided to cast his lot with his brothers who were big, strong and gifted in maintenance work. It must be remembered that it was a seasonal operation and any long delays involving the shutting down of rides could not be tolerated. The maintenance crew had to be adept at "making do" and doing repairs quickly.

Another brother, Raymond, became an outstanding and popular pitcher for the old West Haven Sailors at Donovan Field and then coach of the Hamden High School baseball team.

The year 1950 saw Harold reenlisting for a tour of duty in the Korean War. By 1952 he was back and was assigned, in addition to his other duties, to perform all electrical maintenance at the automobile race track. It was also vital for him to keep on making spare parts for emergency repairs.

Part of his innovative genius came to light when he gave movement to a heretofore immobile figure known as the "Laughing Lady" a seven foot figure set in a glass cubicle on the facade of Death Valley, a fun house.

Even today, when the other old timers get together and start to reminisce about the "good old days," someone is sure to recall that when one of the mechanical or electrical malfunctions at the Rock required an immediate "quick fix," it brought forth the rallying cry of:

"GO GET THE HARTMANNS!"

Harold Hartmann working the Ferris Wheel at Savin Rock, 1941.

This cannon was found 1500 feet off shore opposite Morgan Street in 1937 by Harold Hartmann, then 17, and his brother Earl, then 15. The iron gun is believed to be a relic of the British landing party at West Haven during the Revolutionary War.

Turk's Restaurant, East side of Rock Street between Jimmie's and the Italian Villa, 1941.

Ray Ramadon of Turks Restaurant, 25 Rock Street. circa 1941.

Kohr Bros. Frozen Custard Stand, Northwest corner of Beach and Grove Streets around 1948.

Don Cameron's Collection

Carl's was located at 505 Beach Street, at the entrance to the Midway and was succeeded by Pat's (Libero) Stand. A frozen custard was a favorite at the Rock, 1938.

The Honeymoon Express was a sight-seeing train ride of the area. White City, 1940.

Diane Dorman in the Kiddy Park, Upper Grove in 1949.

Some brave Thunderbolt/Giant Flyer riders in 1948. A view from the remnant of Wilcox's Pier.

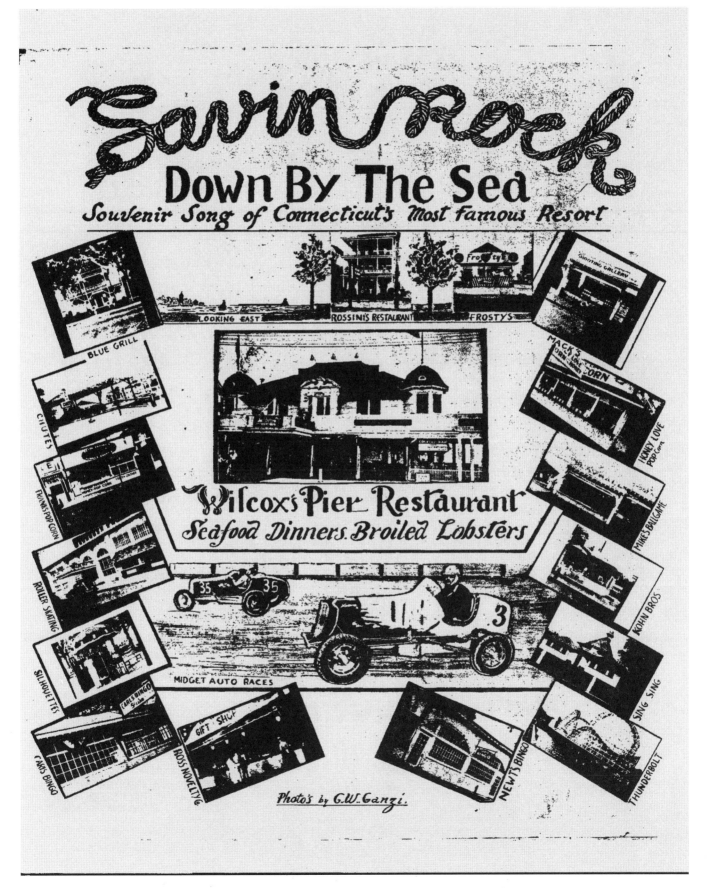

2

free — you will find all your troub les will go up in bub bles at Sav in Rock down by the Sea
-gree you — can get nic ely tanned as you loll on the sand at Sav in Rock down by the Sea
me — There's a ball game each Sun day for that's the big fun day at savin Rock down by the sea
repeat 2nd chorus

Chorus

you can go in Sea bath ing the wat er is fine Lots of nice places To dance and to dine
you can ride on the Light ening bug ov er the humps Skoot on the Skoot er look out for the bumps

Vir gin ia Reel it will give you a thrill Lots of fun rid ing down thru the old mill
Bing at the Bin go and all kinds of games Stroll on the prom en ade eye the swell dames

Coast on the Thun der bolt its a long ride up and down hill with your girl by your side
Shoot down the Chutes but you must hold on tight am a teur box ing on each Tues day nite

3

Roll on the roller skates on the smooth floor   you will enjoy it and come back for more
Sail on the seaplane way up in the air   Rides for the kiddies all hand led with care

a fine holiday you can spend merrily   at Savin Rock down by the Sea
These and lots others there surely will be   at Savin Rock down by the Sea

Thompson's Showboat on Beach Street, 1944. Charlie Coleman played piano, sang and told jokes.

The Showboat's over-the-counter service.

Thompson's showboat Fire, 1944.

A view of the Showboat fire
taken from the beach area.

Fighting the Showboat fire on January 4, 1944.

Weary West Haven firemen shown wetting down the remains of Thompson's Showboat.

Terry's Honey-Dew Popcorn was located at 531 Beach Street.

Terry's Honey-Dew Popcorn

Andrew C. (Terry) Terraciano and
Bob Shaw, February, 1945. Bob
worked for Terry for years and was
an ex-Connecticut state pool
champion.

Walter, Andrew C. Terraciano and Mildred Kozlowski, 1950.
Terry's Honey-Dew Popcorn.

**Catherine, Bill and Diane Dorman in
front of Terry's Honey-Dew Popcorn
Stand on Beach Street, 1952.**

The Italian Villa, a popular eatery, which moved to a spot on Campbell Avenue above York Street because of Redevelopment, but failed there. circa 1963.

"Sloppy Joe's, the home of the famous "Orange Julius" drink on Beach Street. Some years before, there was one at the southwest corner of Church and Chapel Streets in New Haven.

Phyllis's Restaurant, 26 Rock Street, 1946.

The Sea Grill Restaurant, 516 Beach Street, a bit east of the Thunderbolt, 1946.

Northwest corner of Beach and Oak Streets. App's was an "in" place for politicians and Thursday night was a sort of unofficial gathering of "the boys." Redevelopment forced a move to Captain Thomas Blvd., where the old App's name is still magic to hungry and thirsty citizenry.

A 1948 photo of The Sea Isle Restaurant, located at 30 Rock Street. It was a really nice place that, somehow, didn't last.

Old Skating Rink ~ Beach St at Summer
(Formerly Wilcox's Silent Movie Theater)
(Ended up as Peter Franke's Fun House)

Old Skating Rink which became Peter Franke's Fun House.

The National Guard on duty after Hurricane Donna, September, 1960.

Al Nachand in the control room of Peter Franke's Fun House, 1948.

The Spinning disc. Harold Hartmann 3rd from right, Peter Franke 4th from right, 1946.

The skirt blower, 1946.

The revolving barrel, 1946.

The Virginia Reel, located on Beach Street and Campbell Avenue, was built in 1925 and was destroyed by fire in 1946. It was rebuilt in 1947 and finally razed in 1966 during redevelopment. At different times there was a silent movie theater and a nite club under it.

A close-up view of the Virginia Reel.

Russ Levere's Collection

The Beacon, a nightclub of sorts, was quartered under the Virginia Reel. Proprietors, Ralph and Elizabeth Nastri. Nettie Nastri at the bar. Earlier, a silent movie theater occupied this site. Late 1930's.

A view of the Virginia Reel fire from Beach Street, July, 4, 1946.
William ("Wiggie") Johnson's Collection

The Jitterbug, Upper Grove, was built in 1925 as the "Lightning Bug" and was faster and bouncier than it looked, 1947.

Al Knoxie on left and Bill Moore on right at the Jitterbug in 1948. Both were old Savin Rockers.

The Boomerang, White City, 1948.

The Whip, Lower Grove, near Palace Street, 1948.

William (Bill) Levere with his two sons, Russ and Ron, in 1948. Midget Auto Speedway in background.

The Roto Jet at Savin Rock, 1950's.

Frenchy's Dart Game, Beach Street. circa 1947.

Ernie Panico's Stand on the Midway. circa 1948.

Sam Ross, a Midway operator who
was never without his cigar, 1951.

"Tugboat Annie" Stand. "Stretch" Conte inside. circa 1946.

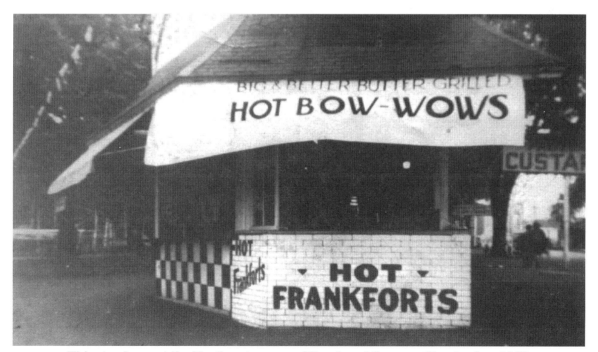

This stand was at the Northeast corner of Beach and Summer Streets. circa 1950.

"Johnny" visits Pat's stand on Beach Street. Pat Libero, Sr., at left, A. D. Cozzolino and Son (Tobacconists) at right. circa 1945.

Johnny Roventino was a pint-size bellboy who became one of the best known figures in American advertising by shouting "Call for Philip Morris" (cigarettes) on many popular radio and television shows. After his death at 88 was reported in early December, 1998, it was learned that there were actually three "Johnnys."
Albert Altieri of Bridgeport was the traveling "Johnny" who performed all over the world and with Bob Hope, Bing Crosby and Phil Harris. A third "Johnny" worked in some USO shows during WW II.

Pat's (Libero) Stand at the entrance to the Midway. circa 1940.

Building of the Sky Blazer at White City. Peter Franke's Fun House at right, 1946.

The Sky Blazer builders. Francis J. Nix is among the workers.

This is the massive wheel that drove the Sky Blazer Roller Coaster.

Popular Club Continental was at the rear of Jake's Hot Dog Stand on Beach Street. circa late 1940's - early 1950's.

Sophie's (Aboyd) Baseball Team. Sophie ran a very popular tavern on Grove Street and sponsored athletic teams. 1957 Photo.

A partial view of the White City from the "Sky Blazer" 1957.

Diane Dorman rides the Carousel, 1949.

Kiddies' Ferris Wheel, 1937.

Scotty's was located just east of Cove River dike at Sea Bluff Beach. A popular snack bar during the latter half of the 1950's.

Arthur Larrivee was the owner of Art's Corner Store located on Marsh and Oak Streets, diagonally across the old trolley tracks from Donovan Field. It was a fixture there for many years. circa 1950.

Kate and Diane Dorman in front of Mike's Restaurant, Thomas Street near Campbell Avenue. Now located at 111 Campbell Avenue and still serving excellent Italian cuisine. 1954.

Old St. Lawrence Summer Chapel, corner of Summer Street and Savin Avenue. Razed during Savin Rock Redevelopment in 1966 -1967.

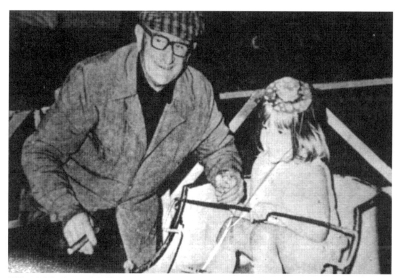

Ray Hartmann, Jr., Kiddy Park, 1940's.

The kids loved Michael "PeeWee" Loretto, who once sold tin whistles at the Rock. When whistles went out Mr. Levere put him on Kiddy Park rides, 1950 photo.

Claude Birchman, a kindly gentleman who was also much loved by tots. Kiddie Park, Savin Rock, 1951.

"Laughing Lady" whose laughter reverberated throughout much of the Rock. One of Savin Rocks best remembered attractions. Frank Cosenza was the man behind her laugh. His voice was recorded in the 1930's and was used to the very end. Mr. Cosenza passed away in 1995 at the age of 87.

The New Death Valley Fun House was located on Beach Street opposite the Upper Grove. The "Laughing Lady" is shown at rest in her cubicle on the second floor just left of the telephone pole. circa 1950's.

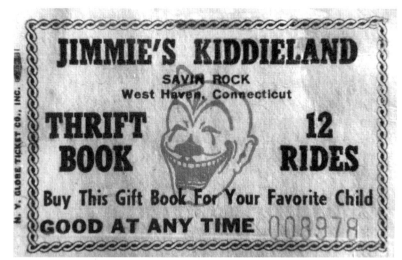

Jimmie's Restaurant had this attraction on Savin Rock Proper after moving the restaurant to this spot from its original site on Rock Street in the early 1950's.

Airplane ride.

Kiddie Carousel.

Beach Street Merchandise Stand with John Assunto, Louis Savarege, Neil Reggione and (Captain) Tony Assunto who later, after the razing of the Rock, played taped music on the deck at the head of Oak Street for the enjoyment of young and old. circa 1950.

Dan Mezzanotte's Stand, 1950. Marshall D'Onofrio at left and Dan Mezzanotte at right.

The Skooter on Beach Street adjacent to Giuliano's Flying Horses. Impelled by the human urge to bang one's skooter car into one driven by another patron, few could resist the ride in the electrically operated cars which could turn in any direction. circa 1951.

Skooter (Bumper) cars, 1951.

As wild a ride as the name implies.

The Wild Mouse, Beach Street in the old Thunderbolt area. circa 1958.

Motorboat Ride in Upper Grove off Palace Street. Kids loved it because they could pilot the boats themselves. 1951.

Skee-Ball, Wilcox's Amusement building. circa 1951.

Diane Dorman playing her "favorite game" at the Rock. After a few paid for games, the kindly owners, Phil and Minnie Garber, always let her play an extra game or two for free and/or gave her a free coupon toward a prize. They said they loved her enthusiasm. 1953 photo. Garber's Skee-Ball was located on Palace Street.

Savin Rock Arcade, South side of Beach Street, in the 1950's All the miniature wonders to enthrall kids from eight to eighty.

Beach Street Shooting Gallery.
Dan Mezzanotte (shooting), and Pete Balzano at right.

Bumper to bumper traffic most of the time, 1950's.

Don Cameron's Collection

Joe Giuliano
Natellie DeRosa's Collection

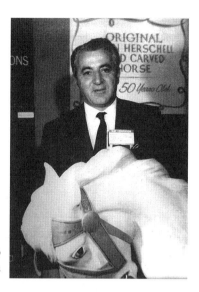

Anthony Giuliano
Natellie DeRosa's Collection

This carousel of 1912 vintage, was built by the Philadelphia Toboggan Company of Germantown, Pennsylvania. Costing $15,000 it boasted 64 hand-carved white pine horses with the larger, more ornate ones on the outside and the smaller and less ornate inside. Its roof's outer perimeter was enhanced by eye-catching rococo styled embellishments intended to create an aura of festivity. A large Garioli organ furnished the music, using two rolls, each with a ten song capacity. The first sound from Giuliano's each day was not carousel music but a bell being rung at 10:00 a.m. signalling, unofficially, the start of the day. After his death, Joe Giuliano's son, Anthony ran the Flying Horses until redevelopment in the 1960's.

Inside Giuliano's Carousel and Arcade, 1951.

The Arcade's Gypsy Fortune Teller.

GRANDMOTHER'S PROPHECIES

Oh speed on, speed on my little **dove**
Carry a message to the one I love
Tho a cruel fate has us two parted
I know that the future has in store
Greater happiness for ever more.

When that long awaited letter finally comes, no words will be able to describe the joy that will be yours. Since you are so clever in so many ways, you have learned to make the best of things. Your life as a result is not spoiled by the curse of boredom. You are fond of gay music, and like to dance. You are an impulsive person, given to exclaim in ecstasy if things please you.

Savin Rock Arcade on Beach Street, 1951.

Ringling Bros. & Barnum and Bailey Circus at Morse Park. circa 1952.

Performing and Working elephants. Ringling Bros. & Barnum & Bailey Circus, Morse Park. circa 1952.

Putting up the main tent, Ringling Bros. - Barnum and Bailey Circus, Morse Park. circa 1952.

Sideshow display, Ringling Bros. - Barnum and Bailey Circus, Morse Park. circa 1952.

Looking about northeast from air view of Savin Rock Proper with Jimmie's Restaurant abutting on its north side, Raffaellis Restaurant to its east across Beach Street. Rock Street, running north from Raffaellis, fenced in Donovan Field/West Haven Speedway eastward from Rock Street with the old Skateland/Arcade to its south and to the far right, Eddie Apps Pizzeria and Restaurant. circa 1955.

Eight mule team advertising Budweiser beer passing by Raffaelli's on Beach Street. Clydesdale horses were used later. Late 1940's.

circa 1952. Beach Street at Rock Street (Hot Dog Row) just past Sippican House at right. Moe's Drive-In became the site of Toni's (one of the Gagliardi's). Savin Rock Proper is shown straight ahead with blasted through road which connected Beach Street and Ocean Avenue where Savin Avenue met them at a point where Bradley Avenue took autos out to the Barnacle Restaurant.

circa 1955. Same general view as above but showing Toni's sign where Moe's had been and Raffaelli's Restaurant at left.

The Trolley Loop area after the storm of 1954.

Bradley Point, South West view of the 1954 storm.

A former site of Jimmies Restaurant, 1957.

Vincenzo Gagliardi, the founder of the
original Jimmie's Restaurant.

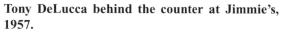
Tony DeLucca behind the counter at Jimmie's,
1957.

Cris's (Crisafi) Band Stand was a refreshment stand on Palace Street in Savin Rock's last years. It had been moved from its last location in the Upper Grove between the Motor Boat (shown just beyond) and the Jitterbug rides. The Skooter and Whip rides had stood on the open lot on the left. Skee-Ball and the old Wax Museum were next in line. Cris's finally became a frozen custard stand and then, during redevelopment, was moved just west of Oak Street where it collapsed through neglect.

Inside Jimmie's, Paul Gagliardi at left, Tony DeLucca at right. Early 1950's.

Earl and Anita Hartmann, Beach Street opposite Morgan, 1958. Raffaelli's Restaurant in background.

Abutting the north side of Savin Rock Proper, Jimmies Restaurant and parking lot are shown on the old picnic hillside blasted out to accommodate them.   early 1950's.

Bill Dorman being served by Lou Gagliardi, Jr., one of founder, Vicenzo Gagliardi's, grandsons, early 1950's. A few years later, over-the-counter sales of this sort were prohibited by the incumbent administration.

Annamae Kearns, her son Billy and friend, Danny Courcey, on the beach at Wilcox's in 1953.

Edward Kearns' Collection

Russ and Ron Levere at Donovan Field in July, 1956.

Sand Pumping began off Savin Rock in the 1950's. Sand was pumped in from Long Island Sound inside the breakwater.

Sand Pumping, 1950's.

Laff In The Dark was a very popular "Old Mill" type of ride on Beach Street. circa 1946.

Diane Dorman getting a free ride from Eddie Stefanoski, a next door neighbor of her father (author) when he was a young lad. 1956.

World's Museum, was located on the northeast corner of Palace Street and Midway, Lower Grove. Also known as Wax Museum, 1960's. Burned in 1966.

Okinawa Beach looking West at Bradley Point, 1966.

Wilcox's Bathing Beach entrance, 1955. Thunderbolt at left.

Surf Club and what remains of Long Pier at left, 1956.

Ron Rohmer, Life Guard at Wilcox's.

These photos are of Ron Rohmer, a Canadian, who came to New Haven to play hockey as a defenseman for the New Haven Blades of the Eastern Hockey League in the 1950's. He fell in love with the area and in the off season became a lifeguard for the Surf Club at Savin Rock. He also did some intermittent radio broadcasting which eventuated into a full fledged radio career. He forsook a promising hockey career for radio and today is one of the areas most popular air personalities with his folksy manner of broadcasting.

Ron Rohmer's Collection

Lenny Jordan, known at the Rock as "Indian Joe," 1955.

The Auto-Cars on Beach Street, opposite Upper Grove. circa 1954.

Right to left: Nine Pillars Restaurant was located at 273 Thomas Street, (now Captain Thomas Blvd.) circa 1954. Waterbury Inn, 283 Thomas Street, Phoenix Club, 287 Thomas Street. All three were year-round establishments.

The Waterbury Inn, 283 Thomas Street, Savin Rock area. circa 1960's. Nine Pillars had just been razed. The Waterbury Inn awaits the same fate.

The State Police gambling raid of July 11, 1959. After this, Savin Rock had to resort to games of "skill" to keep the stands open.

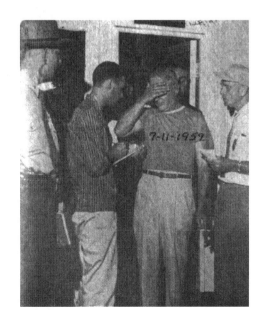

Main entrance to Donovan Field, West Haven Speedway. Savin Avenue at Oak Street. circa 1958.

Checkered flag, West Haven Speedway.

Ralph Zullo, West Haven Speedway, 1960.

West Haven Speedway

Henry W. Dreher's Collection

Smashup, West Haven Speedway, 1960.

West Haven Speedway
Henry W. Dreher's Collection

Henry W. Dreher's Collection

Billy Greco, West Haven Speedway, 1956.

Mark Ferraro's Collection
Courtesy of Billy Greco

Billy Greco wins the race and gives his trophy to a special fan.

Mark Ferraro's Collection
Courtesy of Billy Greco

West Haven Speedway as seen from Savin Avenue looking East.

Henry Dreher's Collection

The Grand Stand of the West Haven Speedway, looking South toward Marsh Street, 1960's.

Wayne Hitchcock's Collection

Dadd's Hotel, looking West on Beach Street from Washington Avenue. circa 1964.

Beach Street near Holmes Street. circa 1962.

Southwest view of Bradley Point in 1962.

The Sky Blazer ran along Summer Street between the Trolley Loop and the corner of Thomas Street and Savin Avenue, 1966.

Bill Dorman takes the last ride on the Skooter Car just before demolition in the mid 1960's. Note his left hand holding the picked up tickets from other lost rides.

Dismantling Giuliano's Flying Horses, 1967-68.

Northwest view of shorefront in 1957 showing partially razed Thunderbolt at lower right and, to its west, the remains of Wilcox's Pier and Restaurant complex, including the Surf Club Beach cabanas. Opposite Wilcox's is Peter Franke's Fun House on the northwest corner of Beach and Summer Streets. Westward is Eddie Apps on the northwest corner of Beach and Oak Streets and beyond the grove of trees at App's west, at the northeast corner of Beach and Morgan Streets, is the old skating rink/Arcade. In the upper center is old Donovan Field/West Haven Speedway bounded by Savin Avenue on its north side, Oak Street on the east and Marsh Street on the south. Visible at the top are homes in the Kelsey Avenue area. At the top left is part of the salt marsh area of Cove River where the present West Haven High School and athletic fields now stand.

Harold Hartmann's Collection

CHAPTER THREE

~~~~~~~

THE WAY WE ARE

Looking west along Boardwalk through grove of trees located south of the old Donovan Field location. Man glimpsed walking is on what was once Beach Street.

Nancy Goudemant was the winner of the "Miss Golden Girl" Beauty Contest held at Savin Rock on September 5, 1971. Nancy is now a teacher in the West Haven School System.

George Goudemant's Collection

Seventeen years later, Nancy Goudemant's daughter, Gretchen Hilary Werda was voted "Miss LittleThunderbolt" at the Savin Rock Festival on June 4, 1988. Gretchen received a sterling silver bank and a teddy bear. Gretchen is now a junior in West Haven High School.

George Goudemant's Collection

Queen Elizabeth's royal yacht "Brittania" passing into New Haven Harbor after gliding by Savin Rock during the Queen's Tercentennial Celebration visit in 1976.

On July 10, 1976, Savin Rock's old shoreline was lined with thrilled and waving spectators as England's Royal Yacht, Britannia, cruised by on its historic visit to New Haven in observance of the city's Tercentennary Celebration. The yacht carried Queen Elizabeth and Prince Philip to Long Wharf where the Queen is shown being welcomed by Governor Ella Grasso.

Britain's Queen Elizabeth and America's hostess, Governor Ella Grasso of Connecticut, 1976.

Thomas Arduini 14, and Patty (Zyde) Gallipoli 16, Cross Harbor Swim winners of 1983.

The year 1901 saw Albert Widmann obtain a charter from the General Assembly to revive the daily ferry service between the Rock and Lighthouse Point across the sound in East Haven.

In 1910 Widmann inaugurated what was to become the annual Cross Harbor Swim. Starting at Savin Rock the contestants ended up at the pier at Lighthouse. He withdrew his sponsorship when the Lighthouse pier collapsed during a race dunking the spectators into the water.

After WW I ended, the New Haven Register assumed sponsorship in 1922 and the races continued until WW II when war again halted the proceedings.

They were revived in 1953 and 1954 but then again discontinued until the West Haven Recreation Department and the Coast Guard Auxiliary Flotilla 17-11 revived them once more in 1977 as co-sponsors. Under their aegis the swim, instead of going west to east, was turned around with the participants entering the water at Lighthouse and swimming the 2.5 miles west to the pier at the foot of Oak Street (a good block longer than the old swim).

SOME SWIMMERS OF NOTE ARE:

Alex Sullivan- Ten-time first place winner between 1925-1941

Buddy Erich- Five-time first place winner (1934-1938)

Sue Slaven- Holds overall women's record for Lighthouse to Savin Rock in 1978.

Gus Langner- After securing first place in the 1926 race at 23 years of age, Gus became the oldest contestant on record to enter and complete the cross harbor swim in the 1980's. He then went on to hold 18 world records in U.S. Masters Swimming events. In July 1998, at the age of 94, he became the oldest person to swim an 800 meter freestyle event held in Wallingford.

Thomas Arduini- Holds the record as the youngest overall winner, despite very choppy seas, in 1983 at the age of 14.

Patty (Zyde) Gallipoli- After battling the same rough water in 1983, she placed second at the age of 16. Patty was the overall winner in 1982.

Mother/Son- The only mother and son winners in the event's long history are **Tom Arduini** with his win in 1983 and his mother, **Diane**, who became her age group winner in 1985.

In 1996, the swim was modified to go parallel to West Haven beaches. Starting at Tyler Street, the swimmers now race to the foot of Washington Avenue, where, after a buoy is circled, the race continues back to the pier at Oak Street.

The latest (1998) first place winner of the shoreline race was **Jeff Postman** who has been an enthusiastic contestant in the Cross Harbor Swim for many years, finishing in the top three five times.

Bradley Point as it appears today.

THE GRAND CAROUSEL

BUILT IN 1912 BY THE PHILADELPHIA
TOBOGGAN COMPANY, MAGIC MOUNTAIN'S
GRAND CAROUSEL FOR 50 YEARS DELIGHTED
GUESTS AT SAVIN ROCK AMUSEMENT PARK,
WEST HAVEN, CONNECTICUT.

PURCHASED THERE IN 1971 BY MAGIC
MOUNTAIN, THE GRAND OLD LADY WAS
BROUGHT TO CALIFORNIA AND PAINSTAKINGLY
RESTORED TO THE PEAK OF HER CLASSIC GLORY

THE GRAND CAROUSEL IS HAPPILY DEDICATED
TO THAT MERRY-GO-ROUND WHICH LIVES
WITHIN THE HEARTS OF KIDS OF ALL AGES

Dad gives little Kristin Kearns her first ride on the Grand Carousel at Magic Mountain, 1983.

Fran Kearns' Collection

Giuliano's famous Savin Rock "Flying Horses" now at Magic Mountain, Valencia, California.

West Haven High School Grounds, Savin Rock Festival, 1986.

Despite a very windy and rainy day, many Savin Rock enthusiasts turned out to witness the dedication of the specially equipped spot for the handicapped on November 8, 1986. The spot, located at the foot of Savin Rock Proper on its west side, was made possible through a $10,000.00 donation from the Lions Club of West Haven. Edwin Boucher, a past President of the Lions Club, is shown delivering the dedication speech for the special event.

Ray Arduini's Collection

West Haven High School Grounds, Savin Rock Festival, 1986.

Savin Rock Festival, June 4, 1988.

Savin Rock Festival, June 4, 1988.

Savin Rock Festival, June 4, 1988.
Old Savin Rock Upper Grove area.

Savin Rock Festival, old Savin Rock Upper Grove area, June 4, 1988.

Savin Rock Festival, June 4, 1988.

Savin Rock Festival, June 4, 1988.

Savin Rock Festival, old Savin Rock Upper Grove area, June 4, 1988.

Savin Rock Festival, June 4, 1988.

Savin Rock Festival, June 4, 1988.

Kite flying just west of Savin Rock Proper in Bradley Point Park, 1990's.

Sea gull's Delight. Most any day along the shore people can be seen feeding them bits of bread, buns or french fries, 1990's.

Stormy seas crashing against new seawall at Savin Rock Proper, 1990's.

Folks enjoying the sea breeze just off Savin Rock Proper, 1990's.

Looking westward at Bradley Point from Savin Rock Proper, 1990's.

View of Bradley Point from old "Okinawa Beach", 1990's.

View from promontory at Bradley Point of sandbar segment and Twin Rock after a heavy rainstorm, 1990's.

View east from Bradley Point Park showing Savin Rock Proper, the old Casino building, Jimmie's Restaurant at left and Surfside at 200 Oak Street. Trees at right are remnants of the old Grove area, 1990's.

View of Savin Rock Proper area showing new seawall, 1990's.

Beach view from the south side of Savin Rock Proper showing the size of some of the rocks used in the new seawall, 1990's.

Kelsey Pier at Oak Street. Named for George Kelsey, the acknowledged "father of Savin Rock" as an amusement area. One of four finished in the 1970's.

East view from Savin Rock Proper (Raffaelli's old restaurant site) showing the piers and groins from the 1970's. The gazebo is a 1998 effort and the building at left is Jimmie's Restaurant.

East view from old site of Raffaelli's Restaurant showing a few of the piers and groins which help keep the sand in place and offer many spots from which anglers fish, 1990's.

The West Haven Land Trust Cedar Tree Planting in 1994. Pat Herbert's school kids planting the Cedar Trees.

Waterfront Grille at right operated for many years as "New England Food & Beverage" located at 343 Beach Street, 1990's.

Stowe's seafood, located on the northeast corner of Beach Street and Washington Avenue, 1990's. Photo shows the Savin Rock Condos at the left side of Washington Avenue with Edgewater Towers beyond. Harborview, 140 Captain Thomas Blvd., can be seen to the right.

Inspiration for an idyll - A small grove of trees, benches and a groin reaching out into a placid Long Island Sound. Off old Morgan Street, 1990's.

West Haven Park-Rec Activities Building, just south of the old Jitterbug site in old Upper Park area.

Looking east from Oak Street along the "Memory Lane" Boardwalk, 1990's.

Looking west along the boardwalk at Jimmie's Restaurant and the Savin Rock Conference Center from about the old Morgan Street intersection, 1990's.

West Walk - Savin Rock's Beach Street ran along here. Looking west from just west of Washington Avenue. The buildings at the right are condos and the one at left is the swimming pool maintenance building. The wide walkway is immediately adjacent to the beach and thus affords splendid views of Long Island Sound and its three breakwaters.

Omnipresent sea gulls perched on one of many benches along the Boardwalk. They're tame enough to feed but if one gets too close their instinct for self-preservation takes over and off they fly, 1990's.

Old Casino showing four regular walkers of the Boardwalk. From the left: Peg and Gerry Hoelzel, Betty and Bill Brennan. Old Rock Street area, 1993. Sadly, we lost Jerry in 1996. In recognition of his distinguished service with the 457th Bomber Group Army Air Forces during World War II, a flag raising ceremony was held at the William Soderman Flagpole.

Pat Dorn & Orchestra at the 1993 Savin Rock Festival, old Upper Grove area.

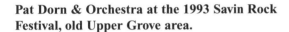

U. S. Representative, Rosa DeLauro, with Betty and Bill Brennan at the Savin Rock Festival in 1993.

Art Gilbert, West Haven's Tax Collector, tries his luck at this stand run by Hymie Schwartz. Hymie was a real old-time Savin Rock operator, mid 1990's.

Mayor H. Richard Borer, Jr. with brother, Tim, at Prospect Beach Fish & Game sailing regatta area during the Savin Rock Festival in 1994.

West Haven Land Trust, Inc. Booth at the 1994 Savin Rock Festival. S.O.S. (Save Our Shore) and IMPACT (Individual Movement For Positive Action) were the forerunners of the Land Trust which is still fighting to keep the shoreline open and free of commercialism. Old Upper Grove area.

Gabe Alvandian and Barbara Barry at the Land Trust Booth during the Savin Rock Festival in 1995. Gabe is President and Barbara a member of the Board of Directors.

Area just North of Savin Rock Proper. Eunice Kennedy, sister to the late President John F. Kennedy and a sponsor of the Special Olympics is pictured here with Harriet C. North, West Haven's beloved Historian at the V.I.P. Clambake on July 9, 1994, Special Olympics.

Mayor of West Haven, H. Richard Borer with Harriet C. North, City Historian at the V.I.P. clambake during the Special Olympics in 1994.

Sue Pimer and daughter Gail Glover watching Mike Pimer building the pier extension landing dock for the 1995 World Special Olympics (they are both direct descendants of the family for whom Bradley Point was named).

Mike Pimer, in the foreground, builder of dock off Oak Street for the World Special Olympics in 1995.

The 100 foot extension, 1995

Savin Rock at Oak Street looking south during the Special Olympics World Games 1995.

Gymnasts performing in the 1995 Special Olympics World Games near the V.I.P. tent.

BRADLEY POINT PARK FLAGPOLE

The flagpole at Bradley Point Park was named The William Soderman Veterans Memorial Flagpole at the direction of veteran Gil Johnson. Private First Class Soderman received the Congressional Medal of Honor, the nation's highest medal, from President Harry S. Truman in 1945 after risking his life in combat in WWII on Dec. 17, 1944 in Rocherath, Belgium. Under cover of darkness at point blank range, Pfc Soderman launched a bazooka shell into a German lead tank. While his company was withdrawing and reassembling, he remained in a foxhole and hit two more lead tanks before being wounded in the shoulder. He became West Haven's only Medal of Honor winner, but always claimed that many who served were heroes without recognition. His widow, Virginia "Ginny" Soderman believes that her husband would be pleased with the many uses and memorials taking place by the flagpole dedicated in his honor. Ceremonies have been held in recognition of Memorial Day, Pearl Harbor Day and many veteran events including honoring some individual veterans. The display of a replica of the Vietnam Veteran's Memorial in Washington, D.C. was a touching experience for the many visitors who came to show honor and respect for those who had made the final sacrifice. The most recent honor bestowed in Pfc Soderman's memory is the 900 ft. sealift conversion ship, The USNS SODERMAN, bearing his name.

Ceremony for naming ship the USNS SODERMAN (T-AKR-299) was on October 25, 1997 in San Diego, California.

William A. Soderman
March 20, 1912 - October 20, 1980

The Congressional Medal of Honor, presented to William Soderman by Harry S. Truman in 1945.

Bradley Point Park Flagpole.   Dedication Day, July 1, 1984.

Virginia Rae Leake Soderman, proud widow of Pfc William A. Soderman, attending one of the many ceremonies held at Bradley Point Park.

Replica of the Vietnam Veterans Memorial Honor Wall in Arlington Cemetery in Washington, D.C. at Bradley Point Park, September, 1995.

Dancing by the Sound

Tony Assunto (Captain Tony) was a volunteer who brought music and dancing to the Savin Rock platform (called "the deck") by the Oak St. beach. Starting with a simple boombox in 1990 entertaining a few youngsters, word of his free music spread and in a short time, he was playing music for over 400 happy dancers of all ages. After his death in 1995, Ramona Cortese, West Haven's Director of Welfare, stepped in to continue the music as a testimonial to Captain Tony. His music still blares out from the same platform enticing all to dance by the sound and to remember Captain Tony.

This tree was planted in memory of "Captain Tony" Assunto in 1995. Wilcox Plaza at entrance to Pier off Oak Street. Tony was also an old "Savin Rocker" at a merchandise stand.

Dancing entertainment from the rear. Savin Rock Festival, 1996.

West Have Fire Department Chief "Wiggy" Johnson making pancakes. Savin Rock Festival, 1996.

The Slide, Savin Rock Festival, 1996.

These three are having their picture taken inside the mouth of a shark at the Savin Rock Festival, 1996.

The First Annual Pound Pals Music Fest, August, 1996.

Alexander Alvandian, grandson of Land Trust President, Gabriel Alvandian at their booth during the Savin Rock Festival in 1996.

At the Savin Rock Festival in 1996, a little future "Dale Evans" enjoys a pony ride sponsored by the West Haven Junior Woman's Club.

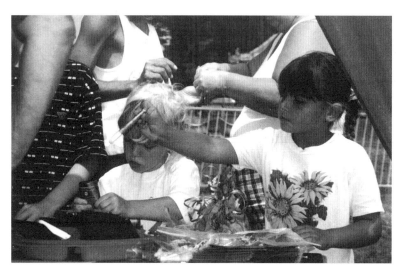

Two youngsters at the Land Trust booth coloring and gluing. Savin Rock Festival, 1996.

A carousel and swing ride, 1996 Savin Rock Festival.

The Author is shown standing on what looks like the bull's-eye of a target. It is actually the markings left from the old Jitterbug ride once located in the center of the Upper Grove between Beach and Palace Streets.

Eric Pimer, of the West Haven Police Department Bike Squad, patrols Savin Rock during the Festival in 1997.

August, 1998. Alongside the Boardwalk, Upper Grove area. Bocci Court was named in honor of "Mr. Bocci," John Barone.

John Barone brought his idea of a bocci court for West Haven Seniors to the attention of the then Mayor Lawrence Minichino who was receptive to the suggestion. In 1984, the city constructed the court near the Wilcox (Oak Street) pier. It was, and still is, filled from morning to night with competing bocci players. On August 1, 1998, a wooden plaque was erected at the beachside court in honor of John Barone. Although a stroke has caused 84 year old Barone to lose much of the mobility from his throwing arm, he manages to keep tabs on the bocci games and players from a corner bench along the Oak Street beach.

Bocci Day at Savin Rock. Mayor Azelio "Sal" Guerra in the plain shirt, 1987.

The very talented Margaret Tatta and her Senior Tappers brightening up the boardwalk with their artistry at the Oak Street platform, 1990's.

Photo by Donald Akowitz

Ramona Cortese, West Haven's Director of Welfare, stepped in to continue the music as a testimonial to Captain Tony in 1995. Wilcox Plaza, 1998.

West Haven's Commissioner of Human Resources, Beth Sabo, during West Haven's 350th celebration, 1998.

The Grand Opening of the Savin Rock Conference Center in 1997. This building is adjacent to Savin Rock Proper on the West and Jimmies Restaurant on the East.

Don Wrinn, West Haven's perennial Master of Ceremonies, 1998.

West Haven's Ambassador of Goodwill, Donald J. Wrinn, is shown in his position as the official greeter at the Savin Rock Conference Center. The recent renovation of the building with its spectacular view of Long Island Sound has produced a much sought after meeting and social center.

Savin Rock Express.

During the 1998 Savin Rock Festival, shades of the old Savin Rock trolley appeared when a motorized replica of the old electric trolleys stopped at the Savin Rock Conference Center. One notable difference was the addition of a hostess in the person of Connie Sacco, Library Director, who greeted all who boarded the Express. After boarding, the passengers experienced a guided tour while traveling along much of the same route formerly used by the old electrics. George Richards, a retired high school principal and local historian, narrated the tour while pointing out all of the city's notable sites. The friendly and helpful driver, Dwayne Clark, added much color to the tour. After completing a two day stop at the Festival and having been a resounding success, the tour was again reinstated for another two days in celebration of West Haven's 350th Anniversary. It proved it had not lost its attraction and was acclaimed by all riders.

Ed Kearns and Denise Smith, taking part in the Savin Rock Festival, 1998.

Diane and Ray Arduini, Kate Dorman watching the passing scene. 1994.

"Memory Lane"
Helen Roche; Bill Reed; Kate Dorman; Jim Roche, enjoying the sea breezes at the Oak Street Pier. (Bill Reed's father, Ray, gave motorboat rides during the Rock's heyday). Mid 1990's.

Dayna and Tom Arduini at Savin Rock, admiring the new gazebo after a winter boardwalk stroll, December, 1998.

Savin Rock Festival, old Upper Grove, 1998.

Savin Rock Festival, old Upper Grove, 1998.

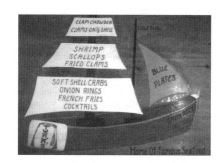

Brothers, Eddie and Neil Ramadon, 1998.

In 1939, Joe Monzeglio opened up Turks on Rock Street. Some time later it was acquired by the Ramadon family who continue to operate it today. It moved to its present location on Captain Thomas Blvd., when the eateries on Rock Street were razed in the 1960's. In the photo are Eddie and Neil Ramadon who, with brother Ray, are always congenial hosts and offer a variety of excellent seafood.

Jimmies of Savin Rock, founded in 1925.

Shown are owners, Jimmie and Paul Gagliardi, sons of Sal Gagliardi and grandsons of Vincenzo Gagliardi, who founded the original eatery on Rock Street in 1925 where the original and much copied split frankfurter became popular. It is now a first-class seafood restaurant.

Subway on the northwest corner of Captain Thomas Blvd. and Campbell Avenue, 1998. This was the former site of the Three Decker Restaurant which was a landmark through the 1960's.

Dunkin' Donuts located on 305 Captain Thomas Blvd, Savin Rock area, 1998.

Biagetti's Restaurant, located on the corner of Campbell Avenue and Captain Thomas Blvd., is presently owned by Linda Biagetti. The restaurant, well-known for its seafood, steak and pasta menu, has been in the Biagetti family for over twenty years. The corner location was previously occupied by Lou Ferraro's Restaurant. 1998.

App's Ristorante, located on 283 Captain Thomas Blvd, 1999. It's former location was on the northwest corner of Beach and Oak Streets, in a converted private dwelling. It is noted for its excellent Italian cuisine.

The Waterfront Grill, formerly New England Food & Beverage, on Beach Street near Peck Avenue, 1998.

Captain's Galley at 19 Beach Street, 1999.

Located at the corner of Beach Street and Third Avenue Ext., the establishment was known as both the Coast Inn and Sea Gull Inn at different times over the years. Its present owner, Paul Patrigani, made bright, new and attractive changes to the building and renamed it "Captain's Galley." It has become a full-fledged and successful restaurant, well attended by satisfied customers.

Chick's, located at 183 Beach Street, Morse Park, 1999.

For over forty years, Chick's Seafood Restaurant, a.k.a. Chick's Drive Inn, has been in business on the eastern periphery of the general area of old Savin Rock. With about 500 ft. of footage on Beach Street in the Morse Park area, it has been blessed, location-wise, by having the Edward R. Warley Softball Field and Little League Complex to its north and a gigantic beach area just across the street southward. Offering more than enough picnic tables and free parking for beachgoers, it has become a favorite place for many bathers, local citizenry and itinerant travelers.

Savin Rock Plaza, bounded by Campbell Avenue and Altschuler Plaza. Captain Thomas Blvd., 1990's.

The Old Malley Summer Cottage located on the corner of Beach Street and Peck Avenue, 1997 photo. For many years, the Malley family had what many considered the premier department store opposite the Lower Green in downtown New Haven.

Southwest view showing the arched walkway between the two main sections of St. John Vianney Church and a glimpse of the senior high-rise at 200 Oak Street in its background. The charming simplicity of the former St. Lawrence Summer chapel has been replaced by St. John Vianney's Spanish type decor which blends in pleasantly with its old Lower Grove location.

Savin Rock Community School viewed from the corner of Peck Avenue and Park Street, 1999. This is the former site of "Oriental Park," a one square block of homes with one common yard and no fences. Their association also maintained a short pier with a clubhouse on the beach at the head of Peck Avenue. (See Oriental Park, page 38).

Strollers on "Memory Lane" Boardwalk, 1990's. The West Haven Park-Recreation Activities Building at right. At anytime of year, in most any kind of weather, people stroll this very long boardwalk enjoying the walks old-time ambience and lovely scenic beauty. The West Haven Police Department Bike Patrol has its headquarters in the Activity Building from early spring through late fall for the peace of mind and safety of all who walk, skate or cycle here.

Looking Southwest at Savin Rock Proper profile, January, 1999.

Savin Rock's own "Old Man of the Mountain" known as "Old Abe" (Lincoln) to many and as the "Old Sea Captain" to others, is located on the northwest edge of Savin Rock Proper. It can be viewed from both the Boardwalk and Captain Thomas Blvd. Despite weather elements and vandalism taking their toll, "Old Abe" or "Captain" still appears to be enjoying the salutes of passersby.

View of profile from Boardwalk.

Savin Rock Gone

A tribute to the era of Savin Rock, the center of immeasurable
days of fun filled pleasures.

A tribute to the era of Savin Rock,
the center of immeasurable days of fun filled pleasures.
Nostalgia creeps over me,
as I look across the empty lots.
I think of what was there and sigh, for now it is not.
I could almost hear the sweet refrains of the merry-go-round,
as it constantly went round and round.
I visualize the hotdog stands,
the charcoal broiling the succulent franks.
I could almost smell the aromas of honey popcorn,
as it was freshly made with care,
infiltrating the warm air.
I could almost taste the variety of flavors
of the creamy frozen custard,
as it was lapped up so relishly.
I could almost hear the popping of balloons,
as they were pierced time and time again.
I could almost hear the shrieks and screams of the people,
as they rode the Thunderbolt,
coming down with a mighty jolt.
I could almost hear the wheels of the whip, as it went flying by,
viewed with awesome eyes.
I could almost hear the thunder of the bowling balls,
as they eagerly operated the derricks in the arcade for a trinket or two.
I could almost see the Stratosphere,
as it looped up and down and twirled around nearly hitting the ground.
I could almost hear and see the throngs of people,
walking side by side to view the sights.
I could almost hear the creaking of the boards of the long pier,
as they treaded on.
Alas, Savin Rock gone but never forgotten
are the beautiful memories that are so dear.

Gloria Romano Rossomando

CHAPTER FOUR

~~~~~~~

AMONG OUR SOUVENIRS

ICE CREAM PARLOR
WILCOXS
PIER
1905

WEST HAVEN
J. Gorman
'98

Jessie Gorman, an excellent "pen and inker," is very well known for her many historical drawings of both local and non-local subjects.

Hotel Ihne dinner plate.   circa 1930's.

Hotel Ihne sugar and creamer.   circa 1930's.

Phyllis's of Savin Rock ashtray.
circa 1943.

Popular type prizes from games of chance
during the 1940's.

Another stand winner.

A small stoneware
jug. circa 1921.

A creamer from The Barnacle,
Savin Rock. circa 1928.

The base of this picture frame was made from
part of the 1870 bandstand after its collapse.

Savin Rock stand prize.

A 1926 Bathing Beauty.

Early on, cops were hired at the Rock
based on brawn and the ability to use
the club when necessary.

A scissors sharpener from Wilcox's.

Keys from Tiernans Old Homestead and the Hotel Ihne.

These were very colorful and popular.

A lighter from Jimmies of Savin Rock.

Various Savin Rock Banners were popular sales items during Savin Rock's life.

A very rare Black Crow Creamer with Savin Rock imprint.

Salt and pepper shakers were among many prizes from games of chance.

The original Stowe's was not in the Savin Rock area but off Main Street on the waterfront. Now, and for many years past, Stowe's is located at the corner of Beach Street and Washington Avenue but as a seafood retailer rather than as a restaurant.

The brass rings from Giuliano's Flying Horses.

COUPON
Star Legion Bingo
511 Beach Street

Redeemable in Merchandise or Certificate
Valued at $1.00

Star Legion Bingo

SAVIN ROCK
45 PALACE ST.   WEST HAVEN, CONN.
SKEE BALL -- POKER
ONE COUPON
This coupon is redeemable in merchandise.
Coupon may be saved.
NOT VALID UNLESS SIGNED
Signature *Philip Garber*

5   *Five Coupons*   5
REDEEMABLE FOR MERCHANDISE

Savin Rock Arcade
474 BEACH STREET - WEST HAVEN

5   Nº B 8648   5

SKATEWORLD
"FREEBEE"
THIS CARD ENTITLES
THE BEARER TO
A *Full* DISCOUNT
AT ANY ONE SESSION

Nº   106

½   COUPON   ½
PLAY BASEBALL • SHUFFLE BOWL • POKER
SKEE BALL • BOWL
COMBINE COUPONS FOR VALUABLE PRIZES
WIN OR BUY
COUPONS ARE GOOD AT ALL TIMES
★ **SPORTLAND** ★
458 BEACH STREET
Savin Rock — West Haven, Conn.
½   ½

BIG HEARTED
SAVIN
ROCK   **max**   GOOD
CONN.   FOR ONE
WIN

Max Gives You More For Your Money

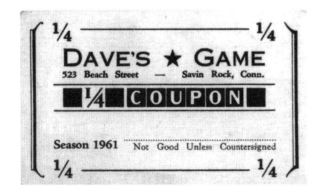

¼   ¼
DAVE'S ★ GAME
523 Beach Street — Savin Rock, Conn.
¼ COUPON

Season 1961   Not Good Unless Countersigned
¼   ¼

THIS COUPON
HAS A VALUE OF
$1.00 **ONE DOLLAR** $1.00
IN MERCHANDISE
or 10 Free Play Tokens

Nº 5467   *Fascination*

POSTCARDS

Russ Levere's Collection

Russ Levere's Collection

Russ Levere's Collection

Russ Levere's Collection

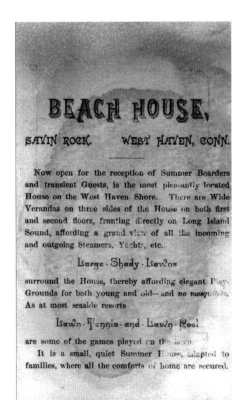

Russ Levere's Collection

POSTCARDS

Russ Levere's Collection

Russ Levere's Collection

Russ Levere's Collection

Russ Levere's Collection

Russ Levere's Collection

POSTCARDS

Russ Levere's Collection

Postcards from Savin Rock were very big in the first four decades but demand for them subsided gradually during the remainder of the Rock's life.

Russ Levere's Collection

Russ Levere's Collection

POSTCARDS

Leather postcards were only moderately popular in the century's first decade, but are now a prized item.

Flying Horses in Railroad Grove, Savin Rock, Conn.

Flying Horses, Railroad Grove. circa 1916.
Russ Levere's Collection

The Whip, just off Palace Street, 1926.
Russ Levere's Collection

POSTCARDS

Typical theater offering of Mardi Gras years, 1911 - 1912.

Russ Levere's Collection

Murphy's Salt Water Pool on Beach Street, complete with bathhouses and water pumped in from the sound. Giuliano's later took over this spot. 1922.

Russ Levere's Collection

Cox's Inn - "Automobile Headquarters," 1921 - 1922.

Russ Levere's Collection

POSTCARDS

Part of Railroad (Lower) Grove. circa 1920's.
Ira Seskin's Collection

Sea View Hotel, Beach Street near Midway. circa 1904 - 1908.

Ira Seskin's Collection

A typical crowd at Savin Rock during the first decade of the century.

Russ Levere's Collection

POSTCARDS

Bus from Bridgeport to Savin Rock, early teens.

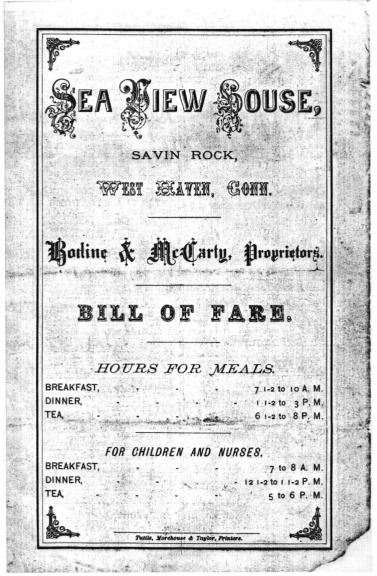

SEA VIEW HOUSE,

SAVIN ROCK,

WEST HAVEN, CONN.

Bodine & McCarty, Proprietors.

BILL OF FARE.

HOURS FOR MEALS.

BREAKFAST,	7 1-2 to 10 A. M.
DINNER,	1 1-2 to 3 P. M.
TEA,	6 1-2 to 8 P. M.

FOR CHILDREN AND NURSES.

BREAKFAST,	7 to 8 A. M.
DINNER,	12 1-2 to 1 1-2 P. M.
TEA,	5 to 6 P. M.

Tuttle, Morehouse & Taylor, Printers.

Russ Levere's Collection

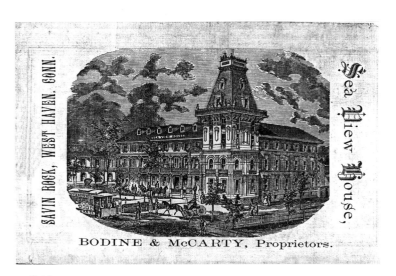

SAVIN ROCK, WEST HAVEN, CONN.

Sea View House,

BODINE & McCARTY, Proprietors.

1921 ad.

Johnny Mack ad.

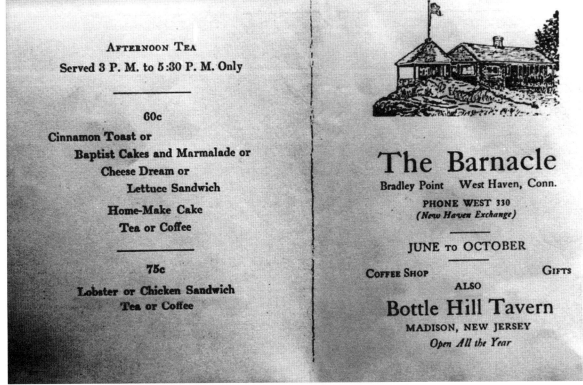

AFTERNOON TEA
Served 3 P. M. to 5:30 P. M. Only

60c

Cinnamon Toast or
Baptist Cakes and Marmalade or
Cheese Dream or
Lettuce Sandwich

Home-Make Cake
Tea or Coffee

75c

Lobster or Chicken Sandwich
Tea or Coffee

The Barnacle
Bradley Point   West Haven, Conn.
PHONE WEST 330
(New Haven Exchange)

JUNE TO OCTOBER

COFFEE SHOP   GIFTS

ALSO
Bottle Hill Tavern
MADISON, NEW JERSEY
Open All the Year

Menu from the Barnacle Restaurant.

Wayne Hitchcock's Collection

Free Parking Spaces Provided for Patrons
opposite Restaurant and cor. Oak and Marsh Streets

For Our Patron's Comfort

we have installed in our Dining Room the latest type
of Blower Heating System which will keep it at a
temperature in which our guests can dine in comfort
and safety during the chilly days of early Summer
and late Fall.

The four self-operating Stanley Magic Doors
between Dining Room and Kitchen controlled by a
ray of light should be an object of great interest to the
patrons of this restaurant as they were the First Install-
ations to be made in this country by The Stanley
Works of New Britain, Conn.

▲

Private Banquet Rooms Upstairs
For Reservations Apply at Desk

Kindly Pay Your Checks At Table

A LA CARTE SERVICE

RELISHES

Queen Olives	.20	Celery, Stuffed	.50
Stuffed Olives	.20	Sour Pickles	.20
Pickled Beets	.20	Sweet Mixed Pickles	.20
Celery	.25		

COCKTAILS

Little Neck Clam	.35	Supreme Grape Fruit	.40
Clam Juice	.35	Fruit	.50
Oyster	.35	Lobster	.75
Tomato Juice	.25	Crab Flake	.60
		Sea Food	.75

OYSTERS

On Half Shell.............................25

Fried	.50	Milk Stew	.60
Plain Stew	.50	Cocktail	.35

CLAMS

Cup Clam Broth	.15	Clam Fritters .30	.50
Clam Chowder	.25		

Little Necks

Soft Shell Clams

Steamed, with drawn butter .40	.75	Steamed	.75
Fried	.60	Fried	.60
Creamed on Toast	.60	On Half Shell....Half doz. .30 Doz.	.50
Drawn Butter	.10	Clam Cocktail	.35
		Clam Juice Cocktail	.35

SOUPS AND CHOWDER

Tomato or Chicken Soup	.25	Chowder	.25
Misc. Kinds	.25	Clam Broth Cup	.15

FISH—CRABS—LOBSTERS—ETC.

Genuine Blue Fish, broiled or fried	.80	Lobster, broiled Wilcox Special	1.75
Sword Fish, in season	.80	Lobster, broiled (large)	1.50
Blue Fish Cheeks " " "	1.00	Lobster, broiled (medium)	1.25
Filet of Sole	.80	Lobster broiled (chicken)	1.00
Sea Trout, " " "	.75	Lobster, Extra Large per pound	.90
Fresh Mackerel " " "	.60	Above Lobster orders stuffed, additional	.75
Fillet of Halibut " " "	.80	" " " a la Wilcox "	.15
Eels, fried	.75	Lobster, cold boiled, half	.55
Crab Sandwich	.40	Lobster, " " whole	1.00
Soft Shell Crabs (2) on Toast	.75	Lobster, stewed or creamed	1.25
Devilled Crab (1)	.50	Lobster, fried	1.50
Sardines Imp., box	.50	Lobster, au gratin	1.25
Scallops, fried, Tartar Sauce, Bacon	.75	Lobster, (Cut) Saute Meuniere	1.25
Lobster Salad	1.25	Lobster or Crab Meat, a la Newburg	
Lobster Cocktail	.75	(per Portion) en casserole	1.25

STEAKS

Minute Steak with potatoes	.85	Club Steak for 4	5.00
Short or Boston Steak	.85	Tenderloin Steak	1.50
Small Steak	1.10	Filet Mignon a la Wilcox	1.75
Sirloin Steak	1.50	Filet Mignon en Casserole	1.75
Sirloin Steak for 2	2.50		

Steaks, Chickens, Lobsters, Fish, planked for two or more at $1.75 for each person served
The above orders served with onions 15c, with mushroom sauce 25c extra, per person

CHICKENS—CHOPS—ETC.

Broiled Chicken, half	1.00	Pork Chop (1) .40 (2)	.75
Broiled Chicken, whole	2.00	Lamb Chop (1) .40 (2)	.75
Roast Chicken, half	1.25	Ham, fried	.35
Creamed Chicken on Toast	.75	Ham and Eggs	.50
Chicken Hash, Green Peppers	.75	Baked Beans	.25
Chicken Hash with Poached Egg	1.00	Baked Beans with Ham	.50
Fried Chicken, Maryland, half	1.25	Bacon	.35
Chicken a la King, per person	1.25	Bacon and Eggs	.50
Hot Roast Beef, Mashed Potatoes	.75		

SANDWICHES

Ham	.15	Lobster Club	.75
Roast Pork	.20	Crab	.40
Tongue	.25	Corned Beef	.20
Chicken	.30	Cheese, American .20 Toasted	.25
Hot Roast Chicken	.50	" Swiss	.30
Club	.65	Tenderloin Steak	.40
Lettuce	.15	Egg, Fried	.15
Sardine	.20	Mixed Vegetable (tomato and cucumber)	.25
Cold Roast Beef	.30	Chicken and Ham	.35
Hot Roast Beef, Mashed Potatoes	.45	Chicken Salad	.50

Served with toast 5c extra

All Clams used or served here have been bro...
A Large Banquet Room Upstairs can be reserved for Private Parties, Di...

Wayne Hitchcock's Collection

SHORE and MEAT DINNERS

WILCOX'S SPECIALS

With Tomato Juice, Pineapple Juice or Fruit Cup 10c extra
or may be substituted for Chowder or Soup on the following Dinners

M — LOBSTER — **Two Dollars**	S — BLUE PLATE — **One Dollar**	R — DINNER — **One Twenty-Five**
Relishes	Soup or Chowder	Relishes
Chowder or		Chowder or
Steamed Clams	Choice of One of the following:	Steamed Clams
Whole Broiled	Crabmeat	**Choice of One**
Large Lobster	or Chicken Salad	Whole Cold Boiled
Fr. Fr. Potatoes	Scallops and Bacon	Chicken Lobster
Salad	Chicken a la King	Small Steak
Dessert	Sliced Roast Chicken	Half Bld. Chicken
Tea or Coffee	Roast Beef	Fr. Fr. Potatoes
	French Fried Potatoes Salad	Salad - Dessert
	Coffee Dessert	Tea or Coffee
	With Lobster Saute Meuniere or	whole broiled lobster
	Lobster Salad 10c extra	or Tend'loin St'k .25 ex

SHORE DINNERS

A — **Seventy-Five Cents**	B — **One Dollar**
With Steamed Clams 1.00	With Steamed Clams $1.25
Choice of Clam Chowder,	Clam Chowder or Soup
or Soup	Fried Fish Fried Potatoes
Fried Fish Fried Potatoes	Soft Shell Crab or
Tea or Coffee	Half Cold Boiled Lobster
Ice Cream	Dessert
	Tea or Coffee

C — **One Dollar Fifty**	D — **One Dollar Fifty**
With Steamed Clams $1.75	With Steamed Clams $1.75
Clam Chowder or Soup	Clam Chowder or Soup
Broiled or Fried Fish	Broiled or Fried Fish
Half Broiled Chicken	French Fried Potatoes
French Fried Potatoes	Soft Shell Crab
Salad and Dessert	Half Cold Boiled Lobster
Tea or Coffee	Salad and Dessert
	Tea or Coffee

E — **Two Dollars**	F — **Two Dollars Fifty**
With Steamed Clams $2.25	Relishes
Clam Chowder or Soup	Clam Chowder or Soup
Broiled or Fried Fish	Steamed Clams or Little Necks
Half Broiled Chicken	Broiled or Fried Fish
French Fried Potatoes	French Fried Potatoes
Soft Shell Crab or	Half Broiled Chicken
Half Cold Boiled Lobster	Soft Shell Crab
Salad and Dessert	Half Cold Boiled Lobster
Tea or Coffee	Salad & Dessert, Tea or Coffee

Lobster BROILED instead of BOILED on above dinners . . . . 15c extra

75c   NOON LUNCHEON   75c
L
12 to 2 Every day except Sundays or Holidays
Soup or Chowder
Choice of Hot Meat Dishes, Fish or Cold Cuts
Potatoes and one other vegetable, Dessert, Tea, Coffee or Milk

...ght from a section of the Massachusetts or Rhode Island shore noted for its p...
...r Dances, Reunions, or Banquets.   An Ideal Place for Business Meetings or Get-Together Luncheons...

Menu

SAVIN ROCK • WEST HAVEN, CONNECTICUT

Owned by a Gagliardi, this popular restaurant had entrances from both Beach and Marsh Streets.

Dinner Certificate No._____

Presented by the Casino Restaurant

This certificate entitles the bearer to one complimentary Prime Rib Dinner when presented at the Casino on Thursday night _____

Casino

Issued by _____ Date _____ 19___

Dinner certificate from the Casino Restaurant, Savin Rock.

DINING HALL

DANCE HALL

Rossini's

392 Beach Street

Restauran

West Haven, Conn

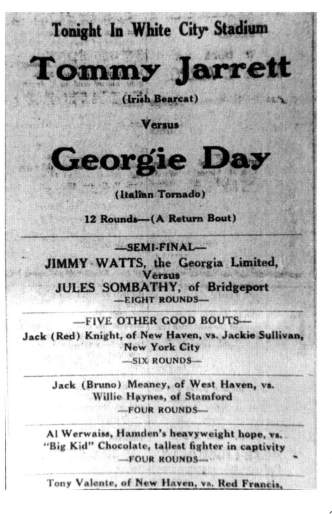
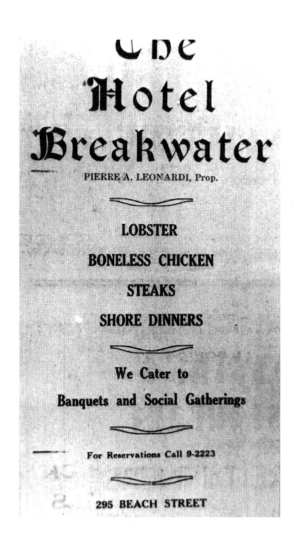

Come take a joyous trip with me,
To a place called Savin Rock
Enjoy its raucous mystery
As we both turn back the clock
In memory down on Beach Street
Let us take a stroll
And if we're lucky we might meet
Pep Johnson - oh so droll
Remember how he hawked his wares
In mellifluous voice
He crooned to every loving pair
"One win - you get your choice"
Across the street the Devil ride
Attached to Liberty Pier
With your girlie by your side
And in your eyes a leer
On that great roller-coaster ride
You'd wait with utmost zeal
For the Devil's steepest slide
And your sweetie's loudest squeal
Of course you knew you had to go
On the old Virginia Reel
The ride would toss you to and fro
But, oh, how great you'd feel
And then you rode the carousel
And grabbed for the brass ring
The horses seemed to go pell-mell
And both your hearts took wing
Perhaps then you would stop and get
A hot dog, coke or cone
You didn't eat with etiquette
But you didn't eat alone
Then a ride on the Jitterbug
Much faster than it seemed
Your coquette gave your heart a tug
As she loosed her girlish scream
After a trip through Death Valley
With sloping floors and such
You kissed her in the alley
And she said she loved you much
'Twas your Eden in West Haven
You thought-forevermore
But now you hear Poe's Raven
As it croaks out "Nevermore."

Bennett W. Dorman

Bill Dorman with his ever-ready camera on the Savin Rock Boardwalk where he claims that if you stand real still and listen carefully, the sound of the carousels and the sizzle of the hot dogs will envelop you.